History Summarized

RUSSIAN REVOLUTION OF 1917

WORLD
BOOK

www.worldbook.com

World Book, Inc.
180 North LaSalle Street
Suite 900
Chicago, Illinois 60601
USA

For information about other "History Summarized" titles, as well as other World Book print and digital publications, please go to **www.worldbook.com**.

For information about other World Book publications, call 1-800-WORLDBK (967-5325).

For information about sales to schools and libraries, call 1-800-975-3250 (United States) or 1-800-837-5365 (Canada).

Library of Congress Cataloging-in-Publication Data for this volume has been applied for.

History Summarized
ISBN: 978-0-7166-3800-1 (set, hc.)

Russian Revolution of 1917
ISBN: 978-0-7166-3806-3 (hc.)

Also available as:
ISBN: 978-0-7166-3816-2 (e-book)

Printed in China by Shenzhen Wing King Tong Paper Products Co., Ltd., Shenzhen, Guangdong
1st printing July 2018

STAFF

Writer: Tom Firme

Executive Committee

President
Jim O'Rourke

Vice President and
Editor in Chief
Paul A. Kobasa

Vice President, Finance
Donald D. Keller

Vice President, Marketing
Jean Lin

Vice President, International
Maksim Rutenberg

Vice President, Technology
Jason Dole

Director, Human Resources
Bev Ecker

Editorial

Director, New Print
Tom Evans

Managing Editor
Jeff De La Rosa

Senior Editor
Shawn Brennan

Librarian
S. Thomas Richardson

Manager, Contracts and
Compliance
(Rights and Permissions)
Loranne K. Shields

Manager, Indexing Services
David Pofelski

Digital

Director, Digital Product
Development
Erika Meller

Digital Product Manager
Jonathan Wills

Manufacturing/Production

Manufacturing Manager
Anne Fritzinger

Production Specialist
Curley Hunter

Proofreader
Nathalie Strassheim

Graphics and Design

Senior Art Director
Tom Evans

Coordinator, Design
Development and Production
Brenda Tropinski

Senior Visual
Communications Designer
Melanie Bender

Senior Designer
Isaiah Sheppard

Media Editor
Rosalia Bledsoe

Senior Cartographer
John M. Rejba

TABLE OF CONTENTS

"History Summarized"

Each book in this series concisely surveys a major historical event or interrelated series of events or a major cultural, economic, political or social movement. Especially important and interesting aspects of the subject of each book are highlighted in feature sections. Use a "History Summarized" book as an introduction to its subject in preparation for deeper study or as a review of the subject to reinforce what has been studied about the topic.

What was the Russian Revolution of 1917?

The Russian Revolution of 1917 was a series of rebellions against the Russian *czar* (*zahr*) (emperor), Nicholas II. (Also spelled *tsar* or *tzar*.) The revolution swept away the Russian monarchy and laid the foundation for the Union of Soviet (*SOH vee eht*) Socialist Republics, also called the Soviet Union. The Soviet Union ruled Russia and its neighboring republics for 70 years.

In March 1917 (February on the old Russian calendar, which was changed in 1918), the Russian people rebelled against Nicholas. He gave up his throne, and a *provisional* (temporary) government tried to administer the country. That government was unable to resolve the many challenges facing Russia. The October Revolution took place in November 1917, when the Bolshevik (*BOHL shuh vihk*) (later Communist) Party seized power. That takeover is sometimes called the October, Bolshevik, or Communist Revolution.

Ivan IV, the Terrible (seated at left of table) in 1547 became the first Russian ruler to be crowned czar. He conquered vast lands southeast of Moscow along the Volga River and opened trade with England. In this painting, Ivan IV shows his treasures to the ambassador of Queen Elizabeth I of England (standing at front right of table).

CHAPTER ONE

History of Russia before the 1860's

Beginning about 1200 B.C., the Cimmerians (*suh MIHR ee uhnz*), a Balkan people, lived north of the Black Sea in what is now southern Ukraine. Around 700 B.C., the Scythians (*SIHTH ee uhnz*), a nomadic people from central Asia, defeated the Cimmerians and drove them south. The Scythians controlled the region until about 200 B.C. They fell to the Sarmatians (*sahr MAY shuhnz*), another Iranian group. The Scythians and the Sarmatians lived in close contact with Greek colonies—later controlled by the Romans—along the northern coast of the Black Sea. They absorbed many Greek and Roman ways of life through trade, marriage, and other contacts.

Germanic tribes from the west, called the Goths, conquered the region about A.D. 200. The Goths ruled until about 370, when they were defeated by the Huns, a warlike Asian people. The Hun empire broke up after their leader, Attila, died in 453. The Avars, a tribe related to the Huns, began to rule the region in the mid-500's. The Khazars, another Asian people, won the southern Volga and northern Caucasus regions in the mid-600's. They adopted Judaism and established a busy trade with other peoples.

By the 800's, Slavic groups had built many towns in eastern Europe, including what became the European part of Russia. They had also developed an active trade. No one knows where the Slavs came from. Some historians believe they came in the 400's from the area that is now Poland. Others think the Slavs were farmers in the Black Sea region under Scythian rule or earlier. Slavs of what are now Belarus, Russia, and Ukraine became known as East Slavs.

The earliest written Russian history of the 800's is the *Primary Chronicle*, written in Kiev (*KEE ehf* or *kee EHV*), probably in 1111. It says that quarreling Slavic groups in the town of Novgorod (*NAWV guh ruht*) (now Velikiy Novgorod [*vyih LEE kee yuh NAWV guh ruht*]) asked a Viking tribe to rule them and bring order to the land. The Vikings were called the Varangian Russes. Historians who accept the *Primary Chronicle* as true believe that Russia took its name from this tribe. According to the *Primary Chronicle,* a group of related Varangian families headed by a prince named Rurik arrived in 862. Rurik settled in Novgorod, and the area became known as the "land of the Rus."

Many historians doubt that the Slavs of Novgorod invited the Vikings to rule them. They believe the Vikings invaded the region. Some historians claim the word *Rus*, from which Russia took its name, was the name of an early Slavic tribe in the Black Sea region. It is known, however, that the first state founded by East Slavs—called Kievan Rus—was established at present-day Kiev in the 800's. Kiev, now the capital of Ukraine, was an important trading center on the Dnieper River. Whether it had been developed by the Vikings is unclear.

The state of Kievan Rus

The *Primary Chronicle* states that Oleg, a Varangian, captured Kiev in 882 and ruled as its prince. During the 900's, the other *principalities* (regions ruled by a prince) of Kievan Rus recognized Kiev's importance. Kiev lay on the main trade route connecting the Baltic Sea with the Black Sea and the Byzantine Empire. In addition, Kiev's forces defended Kievan Rus against invading tribes from the south and east. The ruler of Kiev came to be called *grand prince* and ranked above the other princes of Kievan Rus.

About 988, Grand Prince Vladimir I (*Volodymyr* in Ukrainian) (956?-1015) became a Christian. At that time, the East Slavs worshiped the forces of nature. Vladimir made Christianity the state religion, and most people under his rule turned Christian. Vladimir later became a saint of the Russian Orthodox Church.

Several grand princes were strong rulers, but Kiev's power began to decrease after the mid-1000's. The rulers of other Kievan Rus principalities grew in power, and they fought many destructive wars. In Novgorod and a few other towns with strong local governments, the princes were driven out. Badly weakened by civil wars and without strong central control, Kievan Rus fell to huge armies of Mongols (*MONG guhlz*) called *Tatars* (*TAH tuhrz*), or *Tartars* (*TAHR tuhrz*), who swept across Russia from the east during the 1200's.

Mongol rule

In 1237, Batu, a grandson of the conqueror Genghis Khan (*JEHNG gihs KAHN*) (1162?-1227), led between 150,000 and 200,000 Mongol troops into Russia. The Mongols destroyed one Russian town after another. In 1240, they destroyed Kiev, and Russia became part of the Mongol Empire. It was included in a section called the Golden Horde. The capital of the Golden Horde was at Sarai, near what is now Volgograd (*VOL guh grad* or *VOHL guh grad*).

Batu forced the surviving Russian princes to pledge allegiance to the Golden Horde and to pay heavy taxes. From time to time, the Mongols left their capital and wiped out the people of various areas because of their disloyalty. The Mongols also appointed the Russian grand prince and forced many Russians to serve in their armies. But they interfered little with Russian life in general. The Mongols were chiefly interested in maintaining their power and collecting taxes.

During the period of Mongol rule, which ended in the late 1400's, the new ideas and reforming spirit of the Renaissance (*REHN uh sahns*) were dramatically changing many aspects of life in Western Europe. But under Mongol control, Russia was to a great extent cut off from these important Western influences.

The rise of Moscow

In the early 1300's, Prince Yuri of Moscow married the sister of the Golden Horde's *khan* (ruler). Yuri was appointed the Russian grand prince about 1318. Mongol troops helped him put down threats to his leadership from other principalities. The Mongols also began letting the grand prince of Moscow collect taxes for them. This practice started with Ivan I (called the Moneybag) about 1330. Ivan kept some of the tax money. He bought much land and expanded his territory greatly. Other princes and *boyars* (high-ranking landowners) began to serve in Moscow's army and government. In addition, Ivan persuaded the chief bishop of the Russian Orthodox Church to remain in Moscow. Until then, Kiev had been the spiritual center of Russia.

Moscow grew stronger and richer as the Golden Horde grew weaker, chiefly because of struggles for leadership. In 1380, Grand Prince Dmitriy defeated a Mongol force in the Battle of Kulikovo, near the Don River. The victory briefly freed Moscow of Mongol control. The Mongols recaptured Moscow in 1382, but they no longer believed they could not be beaten.

During the late 1400's, Moscow became the most powerful Russian city. Ivan III (called Ivan the Great) (1440-1505) won control of Moscow's main rival cities, Velikiy Novgorod and Tver, and great numbers of boyars entered his service. In 1480, Ivan made the final break from

Ivan III, the Great

Ivan III, the Great (1440-1505), was grand prince of Moscow from 1462 to 1505. He is considered Russia's first national leader.

Ivan was born on Jan. 22, 1440, in Moscow. He succeeded his father, Basil II. Before Ivan's reign, Russia was a divided country whose princes were often at war with one another. Russia was also part of the Mongol Empire. Ivan united Russia under his rule. He ended Mongol control of Russia in 1480. Ivan achieved these goals by being a ruthless warrior, a clever diplomat, and a shrewd buyer of land. Also under his rule, the Russian frontier began to extend east into Siberia.

In 1472, Ivan married Sophia Paleologa, niece of the last Byzantine emperor, Constantine XI. Sophia brought scholars, painters, and architects to Moscow, where they helped create a majestic court. In 1497, Ivan issued Russia's first law code. During his reign, he sided with the Russian Orthodox Church against critics who questioned church dogma and wealth. As a result, the church accepted greater control by the grand prince in return for his protection. Ivan died on Oct. 27, 1505.

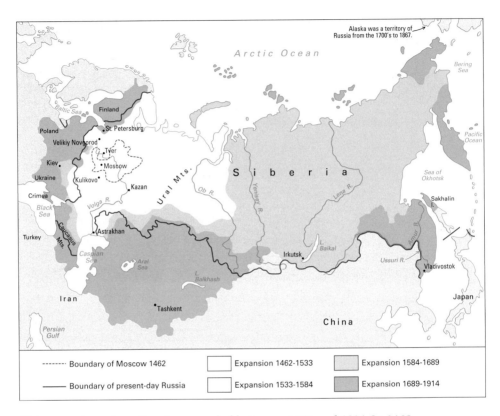

| ------- Boundary of Moscow 1462 | Expansion 1462-1533 | Expansion 1584-1689 |
| ------ Boundary of present-day Russia | Expansion 1533-1584 | Expansion 1689-1914 |

This map shows how Russia expanded between 1462 and 1914. In 1462, Russia consisted of Moscow and the surrounding territories out to Finland in the north and the Ural Mountains in the east. From the 1400's to the 1900's, Russia gained new lands through wars, conquests, and annexations. By 1914, Russia controlled lands that extended from the Baltic Sea and Black Sea in the west to the Pacific Ocean in the east.

Mongol control by refusing to pay taxes to the Golden Horde. Mongol troops moved toward Moscow but turned back to defend their capital from Russian attack.

The first czar

After the rise of Moscow, its grand prince came to be called *czar*. In

Ivan IV, the Terrible

Ivan IV, the Terrible (1530-1584), in 1547 became the first Russian ruler to be crowned czar. Known for his cruelty, he created a stronger and more centralized government and expanded Russia's territory.

Ivan was born on Aug. 25, 1530. His grandfather was Grand Prince Ivan III of Moscow, who was also known as Ivan the Great. Ivan IV became grand prince in 1533 after his father, Basil III, died. Ivan was only 3 years old at the time, and for a number of years nobles fought to control the government.

After Ivan began to rule independently in 1547, he conquered vast lands southeast of Moscow along the Volga River and opened trade with England. In the 1560's, he established his personal, arbitrary rule over much of Russia. His political police terrorized nobles, merchants, and peasants. Ivan's laws helped bind many peasants to the land as serfs. In the 1580's, Russia's Stroganov family sponsored the conquest of western Siberia and gave it to Ivan to add to the realm. Ivan died on March 18, 1584.

Russo-Turkish wars

Russo-Turkish wars were a series of conflicts between the Russian Empire and the Ottoman (*OT uh muhn*) Empire, which was based in what is now Turkey. From the 1400's to the 1900's, these two empires engaged in nearly constant warfare with each other. At first, they clashed over lands that were claimed by both the Russians and the Crimean Tatars, who were allies of the Ottomans. Most of these lands lie in what is now Ukraine. Beginning in the late 1600's, Russian advances into Ottoman territory on the Black Sea and in southeastern Europe caused further fighting between the empires.

Peter the Great and then Catherine the Great of Russia each fought successful wars against the Ottomans. During the late 1600's, Peter forced them out of most of present-day Ukraine. During the 1700's, Catherine's armies conquered the Crimea, a peninsula that extends from southern Ukraine, and completed the opening of the southern lands to Russian settlement. Catherine also forced the Ottomans to allow Russian merchant vessels to sail the Black Sea.

Russia and Austria allied themselves against the Ottoman Empire during a war fought from 1736 to 1739. They also formed an alliance against the Ottomans in the two Russo-Turkish wars (1768-1774 and 1787-1792) fought in the reign of Catherine the Great.

During the 1800's, Russia and the Ottomans fought four wars against each other: 1806-1812, 1828-1829, 1853-1856, and 1877-1878. At the end of the first war, Russia acquired Bessarabia (now parts of Moldova and Ukraine). It also gained a special position in the Balkans, a region that included present-day Albania and Bulgaria and much of what became Yugoslavia. The second war gave Russia

Russia and the Ottoman Empire fought repeatedly over border territories around the Black Sea from the 1400's into the 1900's. This map shows the territory gained by Russia in the 1768-1774 Russo-Turkish War.

control of the eastern coast of the Black Sea. The Ottomans won the third war, known as the Crimean (*kry MEE uhn*) War. As a result, Russia lost its dominant position in the Balkans and Black Sea area. However, it regained these losses after the 1877-1878 war.

During World War I, the Ottomans fought on the side of Germany against Russia and the other Allies. Both the Russian and Ottoman empires were destroyed in the war. The nations that succeeded the Ottoman and Russian empires—Turkey and the Soviet Union, respectively—continued to oppose each other.

1547, Ivan IV, also known as Ivan the Terrible (1530-1584), became the first ruler to be crowned czar. Ivan made the power of the czar over all Russia complete.

Ivan was brutal, extremely suspicious, and perhaps, at times, insane. He formed a special police force and began a reign of terror in which he ordered the arrest and murder of hundreds of aristocrats. Ivan gave his victims' estates as payment to the *service gentry* (landowners serving in the army and government). He also established strict rules concerning the number of warriors and horses each landowner had to supply to the army. Ivan burned many towns and villages, and he killed church leaders who opposed him. In a fit of rage, Ivan even struck and killed his oldest son.

The number of service gentry increased rapidly. But their estates had no value unless the peasants remained on the land and farmed it. Ivan and later czars passed a series of laws that bound the peasants to the land as *serfs* (rural slaves). Serfdom became the economic basis of Russian power. The development of Russian serfdom differed sharply from changes occurring in Western Europe at the time. There, during the Renaissance, the growth of trade led to the use of money as royal payment. It also led to the disappearance of serfdom in Western Europe.

Ivan fought Tatars at Astrakhan and Kazan to the southeast, and he won their lands. Russian forces then crossed the Ural Mountains and conquered western Siberia. Ivan also tried to win lands northwest to the Baltic Sea, but he was defeated by Lithuanian, Polish, and Swedish armies.

The Time of Troubles

The Time of Troubles developed because of a breakdown of the czar's power after Ivan's death. Fedor I, Ivan's second son, was a weak czar. His

Boris Godunov

Boris Godunov (*GOH duh nawf*) (1551?-1605) was czar of Russia from 1598 to 1605. His brief rule was marked by famine and unrest, and it led to a period of upheaval in Russia called the Time of Troubles.

Boris Feodorovich Godunov served in the court of Czar Ivan IV, also called Ivan the Terrible. After the death of Ivan in 1584, Ivan's son Fedor became czar. He was a weak ruler, however. Godunov, who was Fedor's brother-in-law and one of his advisers, became the real ruler of Russia. After Fedor died in 1598, Godunov had himself elected czar by the *zemskii sobor* (*ZEHM skee sah BOHR*) (land council), a kind of parliament with little power.

In 1601, heavy rain followed by frosts destroyed Russia's crops, and famine resulted. Crop failures and famine continued until 1603 and led to unrest among the people. Rumors spread that Godunov had plotted the assassination of Fedor's younger brother, Dmitriy, and that Russia was being punished for Godunov's actions. Young Dmitriy had died in 1591, apparently as the result of an accident.

In 1604, a man claiming to be Dmitriy invaded Russia to take the throne. Godunov called the man an impostor but died suddenly in 1605. Godunov's son succeeded him as Fedor II but was murdered a few weeks later. The invader then became czar, but he was killed by rebels in 1606.

In the late 1500's, a band of Russian Cossacks, led by an adventurer named Yermak (wearing silver helmet and pointing, upper left of center), defeated the Tatars. Cossacks reached the Pacific coast in 1639. By 1700, the Russians controlled almost all of Siberia.

The Cossacks

The Cossacks (*KOS aks*) were a group of elite cavalry warriors in Ukraine and Russia. They became famous for their horseback riding and fierce independence.

In the 1400's and 1500's, most Cossacks were peasants who had fled into the unsettled plains of what are now southern Ukraine and western Russia to escape serfdom or to gain more independence. There, they established self-governing communities. The rulers of Poland and Russia asked the Cossacks to defend their lands against raids by Asian invaders called Tatars.

The Ukrainian Cossacks began a rebellion against Poland in 1648. Tens of thousands of Jews were killed in the rebellion. The Jews had been associated with Polish rule because many held such positions as overseers or tax collectors for Polish landowners. As a result of the rebellion, Cossack rule spread over much of Ukraine. In 1654, the Ukrainian Cossacks formed an association with the czar of Russia. They served in the Russian army until the late 1700's.

The Russian Cossacks played a key role in expanding the Russian empire in the middle and late 1800's, especially in Siberia. They supported the czars with fierce loyalty and served in Russia's army. By 1916, Cossack communities had almost 4.5 million people.

Cossacks formed the basis of the forces that fought the Bolsheviks in the civil war that followed the Russian Revolution of 1917. After the Bolsheviks gained control of Russia and formed the Soviet Union in 1922, they broke up the Cossacks as a distinct group. After the Soviet Union collapsed in 1991, the Cossacks reemerged. They created their own political and social organizations and formed volunteer military units.

This poster questions the Cossack's loyalty to the Russian Revolution. The peasant, soldier, and workingman (in red uniforms, left to right) ask the Cossack (in gray uniform) (translated), "Cossack, with whom are you? With us or with them?"

wife's brother, Boris Godunov (*GOH duh nawf*) (1551?-1605), became the real ruler of Russia. Fedor's younger brother, Dmitriy, was found dead in 1591, and Fedor died in 1598 without leaving a male heir.

The *zemskii sobor* (*ZEHM skee sah BOHR*) (land council), a kind of parliament with little power, elected Boris czar. But a man believed to be Gregory Otrepiev, a former monk, posed as Dmitriy. This *False Dmitriy* claimed Dmitriy had not died, and he fled to Lithuania to avoid arrest. In 1604, False Dmitriy invaded Russia with Polish troops. The invaders were joined by many discontented Russians. This invasion marked the beginning of the Time of Troubles. Russia was torn by civil war, invasion, and political confusion until 1613.

False Dmitriy became czar in 1605, but a group of boyars killed him the next year. Prince Basil Shuisky then became czar. In 1610, Polish invaders occupied Moscow. They ruled through a powerless council of boyars until 1612. Meanwhile, a new False Dmitriy and a number of other pretenders to the throne won many followers. Peasant revolts swept through Russia. Landowners and frontier people called Cossacks fought each other, and sometimes joined together to fight powerful aristocrats. The Polish control of Moscow led the Russians to unite their forces and drive out the invaders. They recaptured the capital in 1612.

The Romanovs

After the Poles were defeated, there was no one of royal birth to take the throne. In 1613, the zemskii sobor elected Michael Romanov czar. The Romanov czars ruled Russia for the next 300 years, until the February Revolution of 1917 ended czarist rule.

During the 1600's, Russia annexed much of Ukraine and extended its control of Siberia eastward to the Pacific Ocean. During this same period, the Russian Orthodox Church made changes in religious texts and ceremonies. People called *Old Believers* objected to these changes and broke away from the church. This group still follows the old practices today.

In 1682, a struggle for power resulted in the crowning of two half brothers—Peter I (later known as Peter the Great) (1672-1725) and Ivan V—as co-czars. Both were children, and Ivan's sister Sophia ruled as *regent* (temporary ruler) until Peter's followers forced her to retire in 1689. Peter made close contact with the many Western Europeans living in Moscow and absorbed much new information from them. He came into full power in 1696, when Ivan died.

Peter was greatly influenced by ideas of commerce and government then popular in Western Europe. A powerful ruler, he improved Russia's military and made many important conquests. During Peter's reign, Russia expanded its territory to the Baltic Sea in the Great Northern War with Sweden. In 1703, Peter founded St. Petersburg on the Baltic, and he moved the national capital there in 1712. After traveling throughout Europe, he introduced Western-type clothing, factories, and schools in Russia, and reorganized Russia's government to make it run more efficiently.

Peter forced Russia's nobility to adopt many Western customs. He also increased the czar's power over the aristocrats, church officials, and serfs. He dealt harshly with those who opposed these changes. Under Peter, the legal status of serfs further deteriorated.

After Peter's death in 1725, a series of struggles for the throne took place. The service gentry and the leading nobles were on opposite sides. Candidates for the throne who were supported by the service gentry won most of these struggles and rewarded their followers. The rulers increased the gentry's power over the serfs and local affairs. The gentry's enforced service to the state was gradually reduced. It was ended altogether in 1762. Later that year, Empress Catherine II, known as Cather-

Peter I, the Great

Peter I, the Great (1672-1725), was one of the most famous rulers in history. A member of the Romanov *dynasty* (family of rulers), he ruled first as czar of Russia and later became Russia's first emperor. Peter transformed Russia from an isolated and backward country into a great European power.

Peter was born in Moscow on June 9, 1672. His father was Czar Alexis. Alexis died in 1676 and was succeeded as czar by his oldest son, Fedor. Fedor died in 1682. Peter then came to the throne at the age of 10, along with his half brother Ivan V. However, Peter's half sister Sophia actually ruled Russia until 1689. Peter's followers forced Sophia to retire that year, and Peter would eventually become the sole ruler of Russia.

Peter had been interested in military matters as a youth. He also had enjoyed spending time with foreign military officers who lived in Moscow, and he learned much about European civilization from them. In 1695, a number of these officers helped Peter lead a force against the Ottoman Empire. Peter conquered the Ottoman port of Azov on the Black Sea in 1696.

Ivan died in 1696. In 1697 and 1698, Peter toured Western Europe with a group of Russian delegates to seek allies for Russia against the Ottoman Empire. Peter also recruited

Western experts to bring modern techniques of engineering, architecture, art, and science to Russia. Russia then lagged far behind other European nations in these areas.

A revolt of his royal guards forced Peter to return to Russia in 1698. Peter crushed the revolt. This victory made him the unquestioned master of Russia. From 1700 to 1721, Peter led Russia in a war against Sweden. When the war began, Sweden was the leading power in northern Europe. With the help of his Western advisers, Peter improved Russia's army, created a navy, and made his government more efficient in raising troops and money for his war effort. By the end of the war, Russia had gained control over important territory along the eastern shores of the Baltic Sea. This land gave Russia a direct approach by water to the rest of Europe.

In 1712, the Ottomans forced Peter to turn over the port of Azov and other territories taken earlier from them. However, in 1722 and 1723, Peter attacked Persia and conquered territory along the Caspian Sea. Peter's foreign conquests helped Russia greatly to expand its trade with other countries. Peter's conquests also enormously increased Russia's political importance in Europe.

Peter strengthened his power as czar and created a senate to supervise the Russian government. He began a policy of appointing people to high military or administrative offices according to merit and seniority. Previously, these appointments were based on family background. Peter also abolished the independence of the Russian Orthodox Church. He also laid the basis for the Russian Academy of Sciences, started Russia's first newspaper, and founded technical schools, a museum, a public library, and an art gallery. Peter died on Feb. 8, 1725.

ine the Great (1729-1796), came to power.

Magnificent royal parties and other festivities, all in the latest Western fashion, took place during the 1700's. The arts were promoted, and many new schools were started, mainly for the upper classes. The Russian Imperial School of Ballet was founded, and Italian opera and chamber music were brought to Russia. It also became fashionable in Russia to repeat the newest Western ideas on freedom and social reform, especially during the rule of Catherine the Great. In 1767, Catherine called a large legislative assembly to reform Russian laws. However, the assembly achieved nothing.

The great majority of Russians remained in extreme poverty and ignorance during this period. In 1773 and 1774, the peasants' discontent boiled over in a revolt led by Emelian Pugachev (*poo guh CHAWF*) (1742?-1775), a Cossack. The revolt swept through Russia from the Ural Mountains to the Volga River. It spread almost to Moscow before being crushed by government troops. In 1775, Catherine further tightened the landowners' control over the serfs.

Under Catherine the Great, Russia rose to new importance as a major world power. In the late 1700's, Austria, Prussia, and Russia gradually divided Poland among themselves. Russia gained nearly all of Belarus, Lithuania, and Ukraine from Poland. In wars against the Ottoman Empire (based in present-day Turkey), Russia gained Crimea and other Ottoman lands. Catherine died in 1796. She was succeeded by her son, Paul.

Paul's five-year rule ended with his murder in 1801. Alexander I (1777-1825), Paul's son, became czar and talked about freeing the serfs, building schools for all young Russians, and even giving up the throne and making Russia a republic. He introduced several reforms, such as freeing many political prisoners and spreading Western ways and ideas. But he did nothing to lessen the czar's total power or to end serfdom. Alexander knew that Russia's military strength and its position as a major world power depended on income that was provided by serfdom. Under Alexander's rule, Russia continued to win territory from Persia, Sweden, and the Ottoman Empire.

In June 1812, Napoleon I (1769-1821) of France led the Grand Army of France into Russia. He wanted to stop Russian trade with the United Kingdom, France's chief enemy, and to halt Russian expansion in the Balkan region. The French swept forward and reached Moscow in September 1812. Most people had left the city, and Napoleon and his army entered easily.

Alexander I was czar of Russia from 1801 to 1825 and a member of the Romanov line of rulers. He became known for his stubborn struggle with Emperor Napoleon I of France.

Soon afterward, fire destroyed most of Moscow. Historians believe the Russians themselves set the fire. After 35 days, the French left the city because they feared they might not survive the approaching bitter Russian winter. They began a disastrous retreat with little food and under continual attack by the Russians. Of the estimated 600,000 French troops in Russia, about 500,000 died, deserted, or were captured. Russia then became a major force in the campaign by several European countries that defeated Napoleon.

Although Alexander had begun some reforms, harsh rule continued in Russia. Beginning in 1816, many young aristocrats became revolution-

Catherine the Great

Catherine the Great (1729-1796) ruled as empress of Russia from 1762 until her death. During her reign, Russia expanded greatly. Catherine was born a German princess and promoted European culture in Russia.

Catherine was born in Stettin, Prussia (now Szczecin, Poland) on May 2, 1729 (April 21 on the Russian calendar then in use). At the age of 16, she went to St. Petersburg, Russia, and married Peter, the weak and incompetent successor to the Russian throne. He became Emperor Peter III in 1762 but was deposed later that year by Catherine and her allies and was assassinated. Catherine succeeded Peter to the throne as Catherine II. She is considered a member of the Romanov line of Russian rulers.

Catherine was a gifted person, devoted to art, literature, science, and politics. Although she maintained extravagant surroundings, she herself lived simply and proved to be a conscientious ruler. Early in her reign, Catherine became interested in the liberal ideas of her time, called the Enlightenment because its great thinkers emphasized the use of reason. She built schools and hospitals, encouraged smallpox vaccination, promoted the education of women, and extended religious tolerance. Teachers, scientists, writers, artists, and actors from other countries moved to Russia.

But Catherine did little to grant basic civil rights to the majority of the Russian people. She tightened landowners' control over the serfs, and she forcefully put down a peasant revolt. Except for raising the status of nobles and merchants,

Catherine the Great became empress of Russia in 1762. She expanded the country's territory and encouraged the development of the arts. But she preserved and extended serfdom.

she carried out few social reforms.

Catherine's achievements consisted mainly in modernizing the administration, though she did little to curb its corruption. She also extended the frontiers of Russia. She acquired most of Ukraine, Lithuania, and Poland through three *partitions* (divisions). Her successful wars with the Ottoman Empire gained the Crimea and lands along the Black Sea for Russia. She also conquered Siberian and central Asian peoples. Catherine died on Nov. 17, 1796 (November 6 on the Russian calendar then in use).

Nicholas I was czar of Russia from 1825 to 1855 and a member of the Romanov line of rulers. He became known as the "policeman of Europe" because he sent troops to put down revolutions in Poland and Hungary.

aries. They formed secret groups, wrote constitutions for Russia, and prepared to revolt. Alexander died in 1825, and Nicholas I (1796-1855) became czar. In December of 1825, a group of revolutionaries, later called the *Decembrists,* took action. At the urging of the Decembrists, about 3,000 soldiers and officers gathered in Senate Square in St. Petersburg, and government troops arrived to face them. After several hours, the Decembrists fired a few shots. Government cannons ended the revolt by the Decembrists.

The Decembrist revolt deeply impressed and frightened Nicholas. He removed aristocrats, whom he now distrusted, from government office and replaced them with professional military officers. He tightened his control over the press and education, reduced travel outside Russia, and prohibited organizations that might have political influence. He established six special government departments. These departments, which included a secret police system, handled important economic and political matters. Through the special departments, Nicholas avoided the regular processes of Russian government and increased his control over Russian life.

In spite of Nicholas's harsh rule, the period was one of outstanding achievement in Russian literature. Nikolai Gogol, Mikhail Lermontov (*mih kah EEL LAIR muhn tawv*), Alexander Pushkin, and others wrote their finest works. Fyodor Dostoevsky, Leo Tolstoy, and Ivan Turgenev launched their careers. Many educated Russians began to debate the values of Westernized Russian life against those of old Russian life. The pro-Western group argued that Russia must learn from the West and catch up with it economically and politically. The other group argued for the old Russian ways, including the czarist system, a strong church, and the quiet life of the Russian countryside.

Nicholas became known as the "policeman of Europe" because he sent troops to put down revolutions in Poland and Hungary. Nicholas also declared himself the defender of the Eastern Orthodox Churches and fought two wars with the Muslim Ottoman Empire. In the war of 1828 and 1829, Russia gained much territory around the Black Sea. Russia also won the right to move merchant ships through the straits connecting the Black Sea with the Mediterranean Sea. The Ottoman Empire controlled these straits.

In 1853, the Crimean War broke out between Russia and the Ottoman Empire. The United Kingdom and France, which objected to Russian expansion in the Black Sea region, aided the Ottomans. Russia was defeated and signed the Treaty of Paris in 1856. This treaty forced Russia to give up some of the territory it had taken earlier from the Ottomans, and the pact forbade warships on and fortifications around the Black Sea.

Alexander II was czar of Russia from 1855 to 1881 and a member of the Romanov line of rulers. He succeeded his father, Nicholas I. Alexander is called the "czar liberator" because he freed Russia's serfs in 1861. He also introduced local self-government and a court system based on French models.

CHAPTER TWO

Background to the revolution

Russia experienced great changes in the latter half of the 1800's and early 1900's. Nicholas I died in 1855, during the Crimean War. His son, Alexander II (1818-1881), became czar. Russia's defeat in the Crimean War taught Alexander a lesson. He realized that Russia had to catch up with the West to remain a major power. Alexander began a series of reforms to strengthen the economy and Russian life in general. In 1861, he freed the serfs and distributed land among them. He began developing railroads and organizing a banking system. In the towns and cities, industrialization altered the face of Russian society.

Alexander promoted reforms in education, reduced controls on the press, and introduced a jury system and other reforms in the courts. He also established forms of self-government in towns and villages and modernized the armed forces.

Even though the serfs were free, they received little land and were heavily in debt. Many young Russians believed that Alexander's reforms did not go far enough. Some revolutionary groups wanted to establish socialism in Russia. *Socialism* refers to economic and political arrangements that emphasize public or community ownership of productive property. Other revolutionary groups wanted a constitution and a republic. These groups formed several public and secret organizations.

The government tried to repress all these groups. There were four broad types of groups, with some overlapping ideals. *Liberals* demanded democratic checks on czars' powers. The *liberal constitutionalists* want-

Background to the revolution   33

Serfs

A serf was a type of rural farmer who lived in Europe, mainly in the early Middle Ages. Serfdom developed in western Europe in the 500's. At that time, the slave-based Roman agricultural system collapsed, and landowners began to grant their former slaves more freedoms.

Serfs were allowed to have their own houses and plots of land on large estates that historians call *bipartite estates* or *manors*. Serfs had to pay the landlord, or *lord*, of the manor heavy rents. These payments included money, such farm products as chickens or wheat, and a certain number of *work days*. On work days, serfs had to work in their lord's fields rather than in their own. Serfs could not become priests or give testimony in court. They had to pay a fine if they wanted to marry serfs of a different lord. Unlike enslaved people, serfs themselves could not be bought and sold as property. But serfs were not free to leave the manor, either. When an estate was sold or given away, serfs were sold or given away as part of the property.

From about the 600's to the 1100's, most farmers in western Europe were serfs, though there were some free peasants as well. As economic conditions improved in the 1100's and 1200's, many serfs in western Europe sought their freedom. Some bought their way out of serfdom, and some ran away to the rapidly growing cities. Others moved to newly cleared lands where the landowners were looking for free, rent-paying tenants.

By the 1200's, few serfs were left in France and Italy. Most peasants there either owned land or rented it without losing their freedom. In England, several revolts by serfs took place before

A serf was a type of rural farmer who lived in Europe, mainly in the early Middle Ages. Serfdom developed in western Europe in the 500's. In this medieval illustration, a *reeve*, or English chief official (left), oversees the work of men harvesting wheat with reaping hooks.

serfdom ended in the 1500's. Serfdom continued into the 1400's in western Germany. A few serfs there became wealthy and powerful, however. In eastern Germany and Russia, serfdom began in the 1300's and ended in the 1800's.

ed to replace czarist rule with a Western type of parliamentary government. *Nationalists* sought greater independence from Moscow for populations in Eastern Europe, the Caucasus, and elsewhere. *Peasant socialists* sought to start a revolution among the Russian peasants. *Marxists* wanted a revolution among the city and town workers. The Marxists were heavily influenced by the teachings and ideas of German social philosopher Karl Marx (1818-1883).

Marxism

Marx predicted that capitalism would collapse in industrialized countries and that Communism would eventually take its place. He thought capitalism would end with a workers' revolution against the owners of factories and other property used to produce goods and services. In the revolution, the workers would gain control of economic resources and the government.

In the early 1840's, Marx began to move away from a philosophy strictly based on the ideas of G. W. F. Hegel (*HAY guhl*) (1770-1831), a German philosopher whom he had previously admired. He rejected Hegel's notion that rational ideas determined events and instead maintained the opposite, that material forces—the forces of nature and especially of human economic production—determined ideas.

In Paris in the 1840's, Marx became interested in the ideas of French socialists, including Pierre J. Proudhon (*pyair proo DAWN)* (1809-1865) and Charles Fourier (*FOO ree ay*) (1772-1837). A key issue among Paris intellectuals was the plight of the growing number of poor people dislocated by the Industrial Revolution, a period of rapid industrial growth that began in the 1700's.

During the Industrial Revolution, most factory workers and miners in France, Germany, the United Kingdom, and other countries were poorly

Karl Marx was a German social philosopher. He thought
capitalism would end with a workers' revolution against the
owners of factories and other property used to produce goods
and services. In the revolution, the workers would gain control of
economic resources and the government.

The German philosopher Karl Marx and the German journalist Friedrich Engels were active in the workers' movement, and they established an intellectual partnership. This painting depicts Marx (center) and Engels (standing next to Marx) in the printing house of the *Neue Rheinische Zeitung,* a newspaper published in Cologne, Germany, at the time of the Revolution of 1848.

paid and worked long hours under unhealthy and dangerous conditions. To Marx, older explanations for poverty did not seem to explain these new developments. For example, he rejected French socialists' arguments that poverty resulted from the greed of the wealthy. He preferred the more scientific theories of British free-market thinkers, including Adam Smith (1723-1790) and, especially, David Ricardo (*rih KAHR doh*) (1772-1823). Ricardo and Smith had argued that changes occur in society due to the automatic and irresistible forces of economic competition.

By the mid-1840's, Marx had adopted the four basic elements of his philosophy: (1) Hegel's idea that history progresses through a necessary series of conflicts; (2) *materialism,* which maintains that the physical world accounts for everything real; (3) socialism and its emphasis on public ownership of property used for economic production; and (4) the capitalist idea that market forces determine economic activity.

The *Communist Manifesto,* Marx's most famous work, outlined what became known as Marxism. According to the *Manifesto,* which was published in 1848, industrial Europe and North America soon would experience economic and social collapse because of the unavoidable defects of capitalism. With such a collapse, the working class would use socialism to dismantle capitalism's foundation of private property. The *Manifesto* invited industrial workers to join the International Workingmen's Association, which called itself "communist." The *Manifesto* also distinguished the working class from other groups, including middle-class business owners.

In 1848, revolutions occurred throughout Europe. But instead of being led by workers, many of them were nationalist, middle class, or even democratic in character. Nevertheless, they provided numerous readers for the *Manifesto.* As a result, Marx's ideas quickly spread.

Marx's *Das Kapital* (*Capital*), published in 1867, offered a theoretical

The *Communist Manifesto* was Karl Marx's most famous work. It outlined what became known as Marxism. According to the *Manifesto,* which was published in 1848, industrial Europe and North America soon would experience economic and social collapse because of the unavoidable defects of capitalism. With such a collapse, the working class would use socialism to dismantle capitalism's foundation of private property. In 1848, revolutions occurred throughout Europe. They provided numerous readers for the *Manifesto.* As a result, Marx's ideas quickly spread.

explanation of how capitalism developed and how it would be transformed into Communism. In this work, Marx traced the origin of capitalism to the establishment of private *productive property*—that is, property used to produce goods and services. The owners of this property possessed and enjoyed more goods and services than they produced by their own labor. By contrast, the working class produced more goods and services than they would ever own or enjoy. In *Das Kapital,* Marx argued that this division of classes created a conflict that drove civiliza-

Revolution of 1848

The Revolution of 1848 involved a series of uprisings in France, Germany, and the Austrian Empire, including parts of Italy. Causes of the revolution included demands for constitutional government; increasing nationalism among Germans, Italians, Hungarians, and Czechs; and peasant opposition to the manorial system in parts of Germany and in the Austrian Empire.

The revolution began in France in February 1848 as a protest against voting restrictions, political corruption, and poor economic conditions. Soon afterward, the French king, Louis Philippe (1773-1850), *abdicated* (resigned his throne). Liberal politicians then set up a new government called the Second Republic.

The revolution quickly spread to the Austrian Empire and Germany. In the Austrian Empire, students and workers rioted in Vienna, the capital. Elsewhere in the empire, Hungarian and Czech nationalists rebelled against Austrian authority. In addition, Italians tried to drive their Austrian rulers from northern Italy. In Germany, liberal uprisings swept through the German Confederation, which consisted of Prussia and 38 other independent states. Workers in German cities demanded social reform. Representatives of various parts of Germany assembled in the city of Frankfurt to try to unify the states into a single nation.

The Revolution of 1848 quickly failed. In France, Louis Napoleon Bonaparte (1808-1873), who had been elected president, declared himself emperor. Protests by French workers were brutally put down. In the Austrian Empire, troops crushed the nationalist uprisings and defeated the Italian rebels. In Germany, monar-

The revolution of 1848 began in France in February as a protest against voting restrictions, political corruption, and poor economic conditions. In this illustration, French workers burn carriages at the Chateau d'Eu, a royal residence in Normandy.

chies became more firmly established in the major German states. In addition, the assembly at Frankfurt broke up without achieving German unity. However, one major goal of the revolution was achieved—the ending of the manorial system in Germany and the Austrian Empire. Also as a result of the revolution, European rulers became more sensitive to the demands of nationalists and began experimenting with more liberal forms of government.

tion through various stages of history.

Marx thought that all civilizations throughout history had inevitably experienced class conflict between workers and the owners of productive property. In ancient societies, according to Marx, these two classes were the masters and the slaves. In the Middle Ages, they were the lords and the vassals (*VAS uhlz*). In the industrial, capitalist world, they were the middle-class owners of productive property and the workers. Marx called the middle-class owners the *bourgeoisie* (*boor zhwah ZEE*) and the workers who did the actual labor the *proletariat* (*proh luh TAIR ee uht*).

Unlike many other social critics during the Industrial Revolution, Marx did not see capitalism as a moral problem. For example, the English novelist Charles Dickens (1812-1870) and the French writer Victor Hugo (1802-1885) saw child labor, extremes of wealth and poverty, and other aspects of capitalism as immoral. Marx, however, saw capitalism as a necessary stage in resolving workers' problems. He thought that under capitalism, those problems took their purest form and so would result in a workers' revolution leading to Communism.

Marx believed that the boom-and-bust business cycles of capitalism would help trigger the revolution. According to him, occasional overproduction created more goods and services than owners could sell. Forced by competition to be efficient, owners had to either fire workers or slide into the ranks of the proletariat themselves. But with fewer workers receiving wages, fewer people could buy and consume products. As a result, the problem of overproduction became more serious. According to Marx, this spiraling process would eventually result in a swelling of the working class and a shrinking of the owner class until the system broke down.

The working class would then revolt and seize control of the government. A workers' dictatorship would use the government to end private ownership of productive property. Eventually, social classes would disappear. Even government, no longer needed to enforce public ownership of property, would "wither away." A true Communist society would then have been achieved.

Unrest in Russia

In Russia, after a revolutionary tried to kill Alexander II in 1866, the czar began to weaken many of his reforms. The revolutionaries then argued that Alexander had never been a sincere reformer at all. During the mid-1870's, a group of revolutionaries tried to get the peasants to revolt. They wanted to achieve either socialism or *anarchism* (absence of government). After this effort failed, a terrorist group called the People's

Alexander II was assassinated on March 13, 1881, by revolutionaries who thought he was too conservative. He was killed by a terrorist's bomb while riding in a carriage in St. Petersburg.

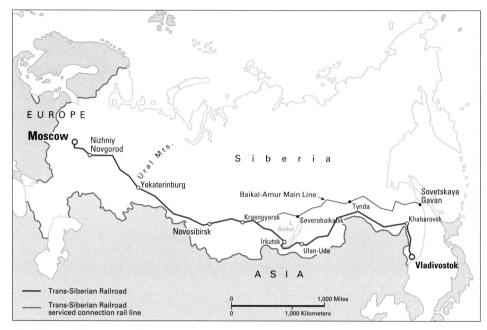

The Trans-Siberian Railroad is the longest continuous railroad in the world. It stretches 5,600 miles (9,000 kilometers) across Russia. The railroad was built in several sections from 1891 to 1916. Industries, trade, and mineral exploration developed along the train route.

Will tried several times to kill the czar. Alexander then decided to set up a new reform program. But in 1881, he was killed by a terrorist's bomb in St. Petersburg.

Alexander III (1845-1894), Alexander II's son, became czar and soon began a program of harsh rule. Alexander III limited the freedom of the press and universities, and he sharply reduced the powers of Russia's local self-governments. He set up a special bank to help the aristocrats increase their property. He also appointed officials called *land captains* from among the aristocrats and gave them much political power over the peasants. Alexander started some programs to help the peasants and industrial workers. But their living and working conditions improved very little during his reign.

The last czar

Nicholas II (1868-1918), Alexander III's son, became Russia's next, and last, czar in 1894. During his reign, industry developed rapidly in Russia. Literature, science, and other branches of learning also made impressive gains. The revolutionary movement had been kept in check until the 1890's, when a series of bad harvests caused starvation among the peasants. In addition, as industrialization increased, discontent grew among the rising middle class and workers in the cities.

Desire for change among Russians had grown through the late 1800's. While people in the lower class had new opportunities, they were still impoverished and living in destitute conditions. Industrialization brought some progress, but peasants and rural people still depended upon agriculture. The years of dismal harvests hurt. Movements emerged during that time looking for a solution to the tight-fisted rule of the czars. Russia became a surprising candidate for Marxism. Karl Marx had expected his theories to be tested in Germany, the United Kingdom, or some other highly industrialized country. But Russia, whose economy depended primarily on agriculture, not manufacturing, would rise as the first to seriously pursue Marx's ideas.

This occurred during the time when nationalism caught fire in many parts of the world. Nationalism served as a factor in the contending revolutionary forces in Russia. However, two competing segments, the Marxists and the liberals, would emerge as the leading forces in forcing the czar to make reforms. Leaders would arise for the Marxists, although they would spend time outside the country organizing before making their big moves.

Nicholas II, the last czar of Russia, and his family posed for this photograph shortly before the Russian Revolution of 1917. The czar's family included (clockwise from lower left) his son, Grand Duke Alexis; his wife, Empress Alexandra; and his daughters, the Grand Duchesses Maria, Olga, Tatiana, and Anastasia.

CHAPTER THREE

Seeds of the revolution

In 1898, the Marxists formed the Russian Social Democratic Labor Party. In 1903, it split into two groups. Vladimir Ilyich Ulyanov (*VLAD ih meer ihl YEECH ool YAH nawv*) (1870-1924), better known as V. I. Lenin (*LEHN ihn*), argued that party membership should be limited to a small number of professional revolutionaries. His opponents supported fewer limitations on party membership. Lenin named his faction the Bolsheviks (*BOHL shuh vihks*), meaning *members of the majority,* and his opponents the Mensheviks (*MEHN shuh vihks*), or *members of the minority.* The name *Bolshevik* comes from the Russian word *bolshinstvo,* which means *majority,* whereas *Menshevik* derives from the Russian word *menshinstvo,* which means *minority.*

At a party meeting in London in 1903, Lenin's group was clearly in the minority. But it gained a majority vote when seven delegates left the meeting over a disagreement on questions of representation. Leninists then won control of two powerful party organs—the newspaper and the Central Committee.

By the early 1900's, a spirit of revolt against Czar Nicholas II had developed in Russia. The citizens wanted more political freedom, land for the peasants, social legislation and higher wages for the workers, and greater representation in the government.

The 1905 Revolution

Russia's economy slowed and social unrest grew. On Jan. 22, 1905, thousands of men, women, and children, organized by Russian Orthodox priest Father Georgi Gapon, peacefully marched to Czar Nicholas's Winter Palace in St. Petersburg, the capital. They intended to deliver a petition asking for better working conditions and a democratically elected assembly. The czar's soldiers fired on the demonstrators, killing or wounding hundreds of them.

The "Bloody Sunday" shootings fueled even greater demonstrations. The liberals formed a Union of Unions to help coordinate strikes and protests by different groups. In February, Nicholas agreed to establish an elected lawmaking body, called the Duma (*DOO muh*), to advise him. More strikes broke out during the summer, however, and peasant and military groups revolted.

The growing unrest was partly linked to the increasingly unpopular war that Russia was fighting with Japan. The Russo-Japanese War (1904-1905) had broken out in February 1904 after a Japanese attack on Russian ships. The Russian people wanted an end to the war, which ended with Russia's defeat in September 1905.

A wave of strikes that began in September grew into a huge general strike in mid-October that paralyzed the country. Revolutionaries in St. Petersburg set up a *soviet* (council) called the St. Petersburg Soviet of Workers' Deputies. Nicholas then granted the Duma the power to pass or reject all proposed laws. He also granted such basic rights as freedom of speech and the right to vote and pardoned all political *exiles* (people banished from their own land). Many Russians were satisfied with the opening of the Duma, but others were not. Lenin, who had been *exiled* (expelled) by Nicholas in 1897, returned to Russia in November 1905 and called for a general revolt.

A mass strike began in Moscow on December 20 and was followed by strikes in other cities. Soon the strike developed into a full-fledged

On Sunday, Jan. 22, 1905, thousands of striking workers marched peacefully to the czar's Winter Palace in St. Petersburg. The workers, led by Father Georgi Gapon, a Russian Orthodox priest, planned to ask Czar Nicholas II for reforms. Government troops opened fire on the marchers, who were unarmed, and killed or wounded hundreds. The "Bloody Sunday" shootings marked the beginning of Russia's Revolution of 1905.

Seeds of the revolution 51

Russo-Japanese War

The Russo-Japanese War brought recognition to Japan as a major world power. Russia's poor showing in the war sharpened the dissatisfaction of its people with the Russian government. This discontent helped shape the course of the Russian Revolution of 1905. The Russo-Japanese War began on Feb. 8, 1904, when Japan attacked Lüshun (also called Port Arthur) in Manchuria. It ended on Sept. 5, 1905, with the signing of the Treaty of Portsmouth.

Japan sought a settlement with Russia over their rival interests in Manchuria and Korea. But Russia rejected Japan's offers. The Japanese therefore made an alliance with Britain in 1902 and began to prepare for war.

Japan broke off diplomatic relations with Russia on Feb. 6, 1904. On February 8, Vice Admiral Heihachiro Togo's fleet attacked Russian ships at Lüshun without warning. Japan declared war against Russia on February 10. Russia seemed so much more powerful than Japan that most people expected Russia to win the war easily. But Russia had only 80,000 troops in the Far East when the war began. More soldiers and all supplies for the army had to be shipped over 5,000 miles (8,000 kilometers) from western Russia on the uncompleted Trans-Siberian Railroad. Also, Russia was weakened by social and political problems that would lead to a revolution in 1905.

Japan had 200,000 troops in North China, and another large army nearby. Japan lay closer to the scene of the fighting, and its people supported the government. Japanese warships and mines soon bottled up in Lüshun most of Russia's Pacific squadron. The Japanese destroyed most of the Russian ships that tried to escape. They also defeated the Russians at Vladivostok in the Battle of the

Sea of Japan. Russia then ordered its Baltic Fleet to the Far East. This fleet steamed from the Baltic Sea around Africa, across the Indian Ocean, and into the Korean Strait. But the Japanese nearly annihilated it in the Battle of Tsushima Straits.

The Russo-Japanese War

The land war went just as badly for the Russians. The Russians were handicapped by poor leadership and a lack of troops and supplies. The Japanese were trained and well-organized and had modern equipment. Japanese forces gradually drove the Russian forces back into Manchuria and defeated them at the Battle of Mukden in 1905. After a two-month siege, Lüshun surrendered to Japan. By then, both countries were ready to stop the war. The Japanese were running out of war funds. The Russian government wanted to end an unpopular war because revolution had broken out at home.

In 1905, at the secret suggestion of Japan, U.S. President Theodore Roosevelt (1858-1919) arranged a peace conference at Portsmouth, New Hampshire. The Treaty of Portsmouth gave southern Sakhalin Island to Japan and forced Russia to remove its troops from Manchuria. Russia had to give Lüshun and Dalian to Japan and also leave Korea for the Japanese. But Russia kept control of the Chinese Eastern Railway.

revolution. By the end of December, the revolution was crushed. The army crushed an uprising in Moscow and police arrested the members of the St. Petersburg Soviet, including revolutionary leader Leon Trotsky (*TROT skee*). Years later, Lenin declared that "without the general rehearsal of 1905, the victory of the October Revolution of 1917 would have been impossible."

Nicholas and his officials refused to give up much power, and the Duma did not work in the way the liberals had hoped. The czar dissolved the first two Dumas (1906 and 1907) after only a few months. For the third Duma (1907-1912), Nicholas changed the election law so that fewer workers and peasants could vote and so that border regions lost some representation. With the changes, the Duma became dominated by supporters of the czar and less democratic.

World War I (1914-1918) highlighted the weakness of czarist rule. Germany declared war on Russia in August 1914. Soon afterward, Russia changed the German-sounding name of St. Petersburg to Petrograd. The Germans easily overwhelmed a Russian army that was poorly trained and badly led. The war strained the Russian economy, which could not meet the needs of both the soldiers and the people at home. The railroads carried military supplies and could not serve the cities. Shortages of food and fuel resulted, increasing the level of social discontent. Within the army, untrained soldiers became rebellious. Many Russian army units refused to go on fighting the war with Germany.

The influence of Rasputin

Meanwhile, Czar Nicholas II and his wife, Czarina (*zah REE nuh*) Alexandra Feodorovna (*FEE oh duh ROHV nuh*), were deeply influenced by the monk Grigori Efimovich Rasputin (*grih GAW rih ih FEE muh vihch rah SPOO tihn*) (1871?-1916). The monk, who was a Siberian peasant and

Grigori Efimovich Rasputin (with long dark beard, seated second from right) was a Siberian peasant, healer, and holy man. He served as an adviser to the last Russian czar, Nicholas II, and may have contributed to the czar's downfall. He is shown with a group of his followers in 1914.

healer, served as an adviser to the czar and may have contributed to his downfall. Rasputin impressed Russia's church and society leaders with his rural wisdom and religious teachings. In 1905, he met Nicholas and his wife. Rasputin was able to stop the bleedings of their son, Alexis, who had *hemophilia* (a disease in which blood does not clot normally). Rasputin's standing with the royal couple gave him influence over appointments to church and state offices. Nicholas filled key posts with

Alexandra Feodorovna

Alexandra Feodorovna (*FEE oh duh ROHV nuh*) (1872-1918) was a German princess who became the wife of Nicholas II, the last czar of Russia. Her mismanagement of the Russian government while Nicholas was away on military duties during World War I hastened the Russian Revolution of 1917 and the overthrow of the Russian monarchy.

Alexandra was born on June 6, 1872, in Darmstadt, Germany, and brought up at the court of her father, Louis IV, Duke of Hesse-Darmstadt. Her mother, Princess Alice, was a daughter of Queen Victoria of the United Kingdom and Prince Albert of Saxe-Coburg and Gotha. In 1894, Alexandra married Nicholas, who was seen as a weak ruler. The czarina (*zah REE nuh*), as she was called, was unpopular with the Russian court and took refuge in mysticism and an intense belief in the teachings of the Russian Orthodox Church.

In 1904, Alexandra and Nicholas had a son, Alexis, who carried the title czarevich (*ZAHR uh vihch*). Alexis inherited the genetically transmitted blood disease hemophilia, and Alexandra devoted herself to looking after him. She enlisted the help of the so-called *mad monk,* Grigori Rasputin, to cure the boy. After Rasputin's initial apparent success with her son, Alexandra regarded him as a saint. Rasputin came to exert great influence over Alexandra and her husband, and he gained input into important political decisions.

After the outbreak of World War I in 1914, Nicholas had to leave the Russian capital of St. Petersburg to take command of the country's forces against Germany. Alexandra assumed responsi-

Alexandra Feodorovna was a German princess who became the wife of Nicholas II, the last czar of Russia. Her mismanagement of the Russian government while Nicholas was away on military duties during World War I hastened the Russian Revolution of 1917 and the overthrow of the Russian monarchy.

bility for the domestic government. Rasputin persuaded her to dismiss competent ministers and replace them with inept and corrupt ones. The government of Russia broke down and, even after Rasputin was murdered in 1916, Alexandra was incapable of rescuing the situation. After the Russian Revolution of 1917, Alexandra, Nicholas, and their five children were captured by the Bolsheviks and imprisoned. They were shot to death at Yekaterinburg (*yuh KAT uhr ihn burg*) on July 17, 1918.

officials who were incompetent and unpopular. Businessmen bribed Rasputin to gain government contracts and favors.

Nicholas attempted to satisfy the demands of multiple segments of revolting citizens. But even when he gave the Duma broader discretion for lawmaking, many were not content. Their skepticism was vindicated by how short-lived each Duma was and how the czar resisted giving up power. Russians were also suspicious of the influence of Rasputin and the involvement of the German-born Czarina Alexandra in government.

During World War I, the widespread resentment of Rasputin's influence over government appointments deepened. Some opponents accused him of being a German spy. Fearing that anger about Rasputin would lead to the overthrow of Nicholas, a group of Russian nobles loyal to him murdered Rasputin. According to a confession, over the night of Dec. 29-30, 1916 (Dec. 16-17 on the Russian calendar then in use), the group poisoned and shot Rasputin and threw his body into the Neva River. There was no full investigation into his death, and rumors about its circumstances have persisted. The Russian Revolution broke out less than three months later, and Nicholas was deposed.

As Lenin suggested, the 1905 protests lit a fire for the larger revolution to come. The czar's grip on power would loosen during World War I as his government failed to provide for domestic welfare while fighting a costly war that took many Russian lives. Eventually, Lenin, who loomed as a leading revolutionary from outside Russia, returned and pushed the Bolsheviks into governance.

The mystery of Anastasia

Grand Duchess Anastasia (*an uh STAY zhuh*) (1901-1918) was the youngest daughter of Czar Nicholas II of Russia. She was born on June 5, 1901. Grand Duchess Anastasia was killed with other members of her family in Yekaterinburg on July 17, 1918. The family had been confined to a cellar by  Bolsheviks following the October Revolution in 1917.

There was originally some doubt as to which members of the family died at Yekaterinburg. As a result, many women claimed to be Anastasia, partly in an effort to obtain the Romanov fortune held in Swiss banks. The doubts about Anastasia's death have been discredited by a variety of inquiries. DNA tests in the 1990's proved that the remains found in a shallow grave in Yekaterinburg were those of the entire Romanov family, including Anastasia.

Duma

The Duma (*DOO muh*), officially called the State Duma, is one of two houses of Russia's national legislature, the Federal Assembly. The Duma is the lower house. The Federation Council is the upper house.

The Duma was first created in the early 1900's, during the reign of Czar Nicholas II. Like his predecessors, Nicholas wanted to rule Russia with supreme authority. However, the Russian Revolution of 1905 threatened the czar's government and forced him to compromise with political opponents who demanded an elected legislature. The first Duma was elected in 1906, with electoral rules created by Nicholas, but the czar soon disbanded it because he found it too radical. The second Duma, elected in 1907, was even more hostile to the czar, and he soon dismissed it, too. Nicholas again changed the election procedures in June 1907, bringing about a more conservative Duma that served from 1907 to 1912.

The fourth Duma, elected in 1912, criticized the czar's conduct of World War I (1914-1918) and sought more power for itself. Nicholas ordered the Duma to dissolve in March 1917, but the Duma deputies defied the czar and formed a provisional government. Nicholas was forced to abdicate. The provisional government was overthrown by the Bolsheviks in the October Revolution later that year. The Bolsheviks laid the foundation of the Soviet Union.

The Soviet Union broke apart in 1991. In 1993, Russia approved a new constitution, under which the modern Duma was formed. The Duma is based in Moscow and has 450 elected members,

The State Duma makes Russia's laws. This photograph shows the Soviet of Workers' and Soldiers' Deputies meeting in the Duma (or parliament) in March 1917. The *soviet* (council) opposed the provisional government set up by the Duma. This environment, in which both the provisional government and the soviet claimed authority, became known as "Dual Power."

called *deputies.* Duma members serve four-year terms. Prior to 2007, half of the members were elected to represent individual districts, and half were elected by *proportional representation.* Under proportional representation, a political party that receives above a certain percentage of the popular vote gets a number of seats determined by the party's percentage of the vote. Since 2007, all Duma members have been elected by proportional representation.

The Duma has more constitutional power than the upper house in some important areas. For example, it can override a veto by the upper house, and it has the power to approve or reject the president's nominee for prime minister.

V. I. Lenin founded Russia's Communist Party. He led the October Revolution of 1917, in which the Communists seized power in Russia. He ruled the country as a dictator until his death in 1924.

CHAPTER FOUR

V. I. Lenin – A biographical sketch

V. I. Lenin founded the Communist Party in Russia and set up the world's first Communist Party dictatorship. He led the October Revolution of 1917, in which the Communists seized power in Russia. He then ruled the country until his death in 1924.

Lenin believed in Karl Marx's theories. According to Marx, the *free enterprise system,* which is based on privately owned business, would eventually destroy itself. At first, industry and businesses would grow, and the owners would get rich. But the owners would pay such low wages to their workers that the workers would be unable to buy the goods that the system produced. As a result, economic depressions would occur. The depressions would worsen until the workers would revolt and take over the industries. Then, the workers would own the factories and the other means of production, and social classes would no longer exist.

Marx believed that such revolutions would occur in Western nations that had highly developed economies. But he was uncertain if Russia would experience a revolution. Lenin, however, was convinced that it would. But according to Lenin, workers and peasants could not carry out a revolution by themselves. He believed that a revolution would succeed only if led by a small political party of professional revolutionaries. This idea was Lenin's most important addition to Marx's social theory. After the revolution, the party would control the government and build a classless Communist society.

Lenin established a pattern for Communist revolutions. First, he used force and terror to take control of the government. Then, he ruled as a dictator, banning all other political parties and all anti-Communist speeches and publications. After coming to power in Russia, Lenin hoped that other Communist revolutions would overthrow the governments of other countries. For this reason, he tried to help Communist movements in other nations. He formed and directed an international organization of Communists called the Comintern (Communist International).

Lenin was absolutely devoted to his Communist goals. However, he also dealt realistically with the political problems he faced. For example, Lenin tried to establish peaceful relations with governments opposed to Communism if such governments were too strong to be overthrown. He also permitted some private enterprise in Russia. This policy, known as the New Economic Policy, allowed the nation's economy to recover from its depressed state after the Communist revolution. Lenin despised all religions. But because so many Russian citizens had religious beliefs, he did not try to close all the churches.

Many Communists have considered Lenin and Marx their greatest heroes. The Communists of the Soviet Union, for example, quoted Lenin's words as a basis for their actions. His works are studied in non-Communist countries to provide an understanding of Communism. Lenin is often thought of only as a man of action, but some of his ideas have ranked among the most powerful forces of modern times.

Early life

The man who came to be known as V. I. Lenin was born on April 22, 1870, in Simbirsk (now Ul'yanovsk), a quiet town on the Volga River. His

The man who came to be known as V. I. Lenin was born on April 22, 1870, in Simbirsk (now Ul'yanovsk). His real name was Vladimir Ilyich Ulyanov. He adopted the name Lenin in 1901. He is shown as a boy (lower right) in this 1879 photograph of his family.

real name was Vladimir Ilyich Ulyanov. He adopted the name *Lenin* in 1901. The name may refer to the Lena River of Siberia.

Lenin's father, Ilya Nikolayevich Ulyanov, was a teacher who became director of schools in Simbirsk province. His mother, Maria Aleksandrovna Blank, was the daughter of a doctor. She was an educated woman who was deeply devoted to her children. Lenin had two brothers and three sisters. All the children, except one sister who died at the age of 20, became revolutionists.

In 1887, V. I. Lenin enrolled in the law school at Kazan University in Kazan. He was expelled three months later for taking part in a student meeting protesting the lack of freedom in the school. Lenin unsuccessfully applied several times for permission to reenter the university. The university is shown here in an 1832 illustration.

Lenin had a pleasant childhood. He often imitated his brother Alexander, who was four years older. Lenin swam, hiked, fished, hunted, and played chess. His sister Anna recalled that he had no close friends.

Lenin learned to read when he was 5 years old. He was taught by a teacher who came to the Ulyanov home. Lenin entered school in 1879, at the age of 9, and became a brilliant student.

During Lenin's youth, Russia was generally quiet and peaceful. The Russian government was an *autocracy,* a system in which one person holds supreme power. Czar Alexander III had come to power in 1881 after the murder of his father, Alexander II. Russia was rapidly becoming an industrial country, though living standards remained low.

In 1886, Lenin's father died. In 1887, Lenin's brother Alexander was hanged for taking part in an unsuccessful plot to kill the czar. Alexander's death deeply influenced Lenin. At his trial, Alexander said he had wanted to kill the czar to gain "political freedom" for the Russian people.

That year, the 17-year-old Lenin finished school. He won a gold medal for excellence in studies. In the fall, Lenin enrolled in the law school at Kazan University in Kazan. He was expelled three months later for taking part in a student meeting protesting the lack of freedom in the school. Lenin unsuccessfully applied several times for permission to reenter the university. In 1890, St. Petersburg University admitted Lenin as a student, but he was not permitted to attend classes. However, he could study on his own and take examinations.

Lenin received a law degree from St. Petersburg University in 1891 and joined a law firm in Samara. By this time, he was absorbed in the study of Marxism. In 1893, Lenin joined a Social Democratic (Marxist) group. Later that year, he moved to St. Petersburg, the Russian capital at the time, and became an active revolutionary.

Revolutionist leader

In St. Petersburg, Lenin soon became a leader of a Marxist revolutionary group. Lenin had the qualifications for leadership. He was highly intelligent and well educated. His writing was accurate, detailed, and clear.

Between April and September 1895, Lenin traveled to France, Germany, and Switzerland to contact other Marxists. In December, Lenin was arrested in St. Petersburg by the czar's police while preparing a revolutionary newspaper, *The Workers' Cause*. After being held for questioning for more than a year, Lenin was exiled to Siberia in 1897.

Exile in Siberia did not mean imprisonment. The government paid Lenin a small allowance, and he rented quarters in Shushenskoye (*SHOO shehn sky uh*) near Abakan in the region of Khakassia. On July 22, 1898, Lenin married Nadezhda Konstantinovna Krupskaya (*nah DEHZH dah kawn stahn TEE nov nah KROOP skah yah*), another exiled revolutionary. The couple had no children. While in Siberia, Lenin wrote one of his major works, *The Development of Capitalism in Russia* (1899).

In 1898, while Lenin was in exile, several secret Marxist groups in Russia joined and formed the Russian Social Democratic Labor Party. After Lenin's exile ended in January 1900, he got permission from the government to leave Russia. He went to Germany to help found the

V. I. Lenin (seated, third from left) poses in February 1897 with the St. Petersburg chapter of the Union for the Struggle for the Liberation of the Working Class. The Marxist group was arrested shortly after this photograph was taken.

party newspaper, *Iskra* (Spark). *Iskra* was an illegal paper that had to be smuggled into Russia. The editors of *Iskra* also published *Zarya* (Dawn), which dealt with Marxist theory. It was in *Zarya* in 1901 that Vladimir Ulyanov began using the name *Lenin*. Many revolutionaries changed their names to confuse the police. In 1902, Lenin wrote *What Is to Be Done?* This pamphlet described his ideas on party organization.

From 1906 to 1908, Lenin spent most of his time writing revolutionary pamphlets and attending party congresses in England, Germany, and Sweden. Lenin found it too difficult to carry on revolutionary activities in Russia. After two years in Finland, he went to Switzerland and then to France. His main purpose was to keep the Bolshevik organization together. Lenin also tried to further the separation between the Bolsheviks and the Mensheviks. He claimed that the Mensheviks were not real revolutionaries.

In April 1912, in St. Petersburg, several Bolsheviks established *Pravda* (Truth), a revolutionary newspaper that was sold openly. To be closer to Russia, Lenin moved to Krakow (then in Austria-Hungary, now in Poland) and became *Pravda*'s chief contributor.

The road to power

World War I began during the summer of 1914. Germany declared war on Russia on August 1. The Austrian government arranged for Lenin to go to Switzerland, which did not take part in the war.

Some Russian revolutionaries wanted a Russian victory. Others wanted peace without victory for any country. Lenin said that he wanted Russia to lose the war because a defeat for Russia would bring about a revolution in that country. The German government secretly gave financial help to Lenin's party. By this means, the Germans hoped to weaken the Russian war effort.

The Bolsheviks were disorganized at the time of the February Revolution of 1917. Some of them wanted to accept the government of Prime Minister Georgi Lvov (*GYAWR gee luh VAWF*) (1861-1925) and end the feud with the Mensheviks. Prince Lvov was a Russian political leader who became prime minister of a democratic government in Russia after Czar Nicholas II gave up the throne. Others opposed both the Lvov government and the Mensheviks. Lenin, who was still in Switzerland, sought to return to Russia. On April 16, 1917, Lenin arrived in Petrograd. He received a hero's welcome from the people.

Lenin called for the overthrow of the Lvov government and for an end to Russia's participation in World War I. Lenin quickly regained leadership of the Bolsheviks, but he was unable to seize control of the Lvov government. In July 1917, following an unsuccessful Bolshevik uprising, the government was reorganized under the Socialist Alexander Kerensky (1881-1970). On July 19, 1917, the Russian government ordered Lenin's arrest as a German agent. Lenin fled to Finland, and his followers escaped or were jailed.

While living in Finland, Lenin wrote *The State and Revolution* (1917), one of his most important works. He told how to organize a revolution and what kind of government to establish after the power had been seized.

In October 1917, Lenin returned to Petrograd. He urged the Central Committee to begin a revolt immediately. Kerensky's government and leadership were weak. Leon Trotsky, the Bolshevik president of the Petrograd soviet, got control over some government troops. Naval crews also agreed to support the revolt. The Bolsheviks decided to act.

With little violence, the Bolsheviks seized Petrograd on November 7 (October 25 on the old Russian calendar). Kerensky fled. The struggle for Moscow was more violent than in Petrograd, but by November 15, the Bolsheviks also held that city. From this point on, the Bolsheviks controlled the Russian government. They had come to power with the help of a simple slogan: "Bread, peace, land." This slogan had little to do with the theories of Marx. But it had real meaning to starving housewives and their families, soldiers sick of war, and peasants hungry for land.

Lenin the dictator

The Second All-Russian Congress of Soviets opened on Nov. 8, 1917, with delegates from most parts of the country. The congress, controlled by the Bolsheviks, appointed a Council of People's Commissars. Lenin was made chairman of the council and so became head of the new

In this painting, V. I. Lenin is shown addressing the Soviet Congress. At his first appearance before the congress, he requested permission to ask Germany for a three-month truce. He also asked for the abolition of private landownership. The congress approved both requests.

Russian state. At Lenin's first appearance before the congress, he requested permission to ask Germany for a three-month truce. He also asked for the abolition of private landownership. The congress approved both requests. The Bolsheviks started peace talks with Germany, and *nationalized* (put under government control) all privately owned land.

In 1918, at Lenin's suggestion, the Bolsheviks changed the name of the Russian Social Democratic Labor Party to the Russian Communist Party (Bolsheviks). Lenin described his dictatorship as "power, based directly upon force, and unrestricted by any laws."

The revolution had spread quickly in the large cities of central Russia. But resistance in distant regions developed into civil war. In January 1918, Lenin formed the Red Army. It was named for the color of the flag of the world Communist movement. The forces opposing the Reds became known as the Whites. The Whites included revolutionaries, democrats, Russian nationalists, and those who preferred the old government and opposed any change. The Whites lacked unity of purpose and were unable to organize effectively.

The Russian economy had collapsed. Industrial output was at the vanishing point. Agricultural production had fallen disastrously. People in the cities were starving. Millions of Russians had died or had fled abroad. But the Communist government survived.

On Aug. 30, 1918, after speaking to the workers at a Moscow factory, Lenin was shot by Dora Kaplan, a member of the Social Revolutionary Party. Lenin was hit by two bullets but recovered in several weeks. Kaplan was executed. To discourage other attempts, the Bolsheviks executed hundreds of so-called "hostages."

Even during the civil war, Lenin did not lose sight of his goal of Communist world revolution. In 1919, he organized the Comintern to run Communist parties in all parts of the world. The organization also helped gain international support for the Bolsheviks during the civil war.

After the civil war, Lenin took extreme measures to keep control of his weakened country. In March 1921, he introduced the program called the New Economic Policy. This program replaced many of the socialist measures started at the beginning of his rule. Small businesses were permitted to resume limited operations. Free retail trade was allowed again. Foreign businesses were invited to invest in Russia. Peasants were allowed to sell food to private customers. Food supplies sent by the American Relief Administration saved hundreds of thousands of starving Russians.

Before 1921, Lenin had asked the United Kingdom, France, Germany, and the United States for credit, trade, and diplomatic recognition. But these nations were unwilling to deal with the Bolshevik government, which had refused to pay Russia's debts and which favored a worldwide Communist revolution. By 1919, no major country maintained diplomatic relations with the Russian government. But after the New Economic Policy was begun, most European states resumed diplomatic relations.

Lenin's health had been shattered by the strain of revolution and war. In May 1922, Lenin suffered a stroke. He worked on against his doctor's advice.

Lenin was concerned about the direction that the revolution was taking. He began to challenge some basic ideas of the Bolshevik government. Lenin opposed the concentration of power in government bureaus. He also feared Russian nationalism. Shortly before his stroke, he had appointed Joseph Stalin (*STAH lihn*) (1879-1953) general secretary of the party. Now, Lenin had serious doubts about Stalin, who was reaching out for purely personal power.

In December 1922, the Bolshevik government established the Union of Soviet Socialist Republics (U.S.S.R.). That same month, Lenin suffered a second stroke. In January 1923, he warned that Stalin was "too rude" and lacked the talents necessary for party leadership. Lenin planned to remove Stalin as party secretary. On March 9, 1923, he had a third stroke and lost his power to speak clearly. His illness kept him from appointing a new party secretary. Stalin went on to rule the Soviet Union as a dictator from 1929 until 1953.

Lenin died of a brain hemorrhage on Jan. 21, 1924. The government preserved his body and placed it on display. The Lenin Mausoleum, in Red Square, became one of the Soviet Union's most honored monuments. Thousands of visitors daily passed by the glass-enclosed coffin to view the founder of the Soviet Communist state.

In August 1991, the Communists lost control of the Soviet government. In December of that year, the Soviet Union broke up into a number of independent states. The fall of Communism unleashed proposals for

V. I. Lenin died of a brain hemorrhage on Jan. 21, 1924. A crowd of thousands attended his funeral in Red Square in Moscow.

The Lenin Mausoleum, in Red Square, became one of the Soviet Union's most honored monuments. Thousands of visitors daily passed by the glass-enclosed coffin to view the preserved body of the founder of the Soviet Communist state. The fall of Communism in the Soviet Union in 1991 unleashed proposals for removing V. I. Lenin's body from public display. The daily number of people visiting the tomb declined.

removing Lenin's body from public display. The daily number of people visiting the tomb declined. Many people favored burying Lenin in St. Petersburg, next to his mother's grave. Lenin himself had requested this spot as his final resting place.

On March 8, 1917 (February 25, on the old Russian calendar), strikes and riots over food and coal shortages broke out in Petrograd. This uprising became known as the February Revolution. Troops sent to stop the uprising joined the demonstrators instead.

CHAPTER FIVE

Revolution in 1917

By 1917, Russia had lost many battles in what would come to be known as World War I. Unrest in the nation mounted, and food shortages were unchecked. The value of Russian money went down. Early in March (February on the old Russian calendar), bread supplies ran short in the capital, St. Petersburg, or Petrograd. Long lines of women appeared before the bread shops. Russian workers went on strike. By March 9, about 200,000 strikers were demonstrating in the capital. The soldiers refused to maintain order. This uprising became known as the February Revolution. Troops sent to stop the uprising joined the demonstrators instead.

Some moderate and liberal members of the Duma set up a provisional government. Prince Lvov became prime minister. On March 15, 1917, the government forced Czar Nicholas to abdicate. Nicholas and his family were later taken into custody. The Bolsheviks killed them at Yekaterinburg in 1918.

Also in March 1917, leaders of several workers' groups, left-leaning members of the Duma, and some soldiers revived the Petrograd soviet that had been first set up in 1905. The new soviet—called the Soviet of Workers' and Soldiers' Deputies—opposed the provisional government. It became a model for other soviets that were soon set up throughout Russia.

This environment, in which both the provisional government and the Petrograd Soviet claimed authority, became known as "Dual Power." The

In 1917, a group called the Soviet of Workers' and Soldiers' Deputies was established in Petrograd (formerly St. Petersburg). In this 1917 photograph, a group demonstrates on a street in Petrograd with a banner that reads (translated) "Long Live the Soviet of Workers' and Soldiers' Deputies."

provisional government drew support from business people, military officers, and government officials. The Soviet had support among industrial workers and enlisted soldiers.

Lenin, who had lived in Switzerland since 1914, returned to Petrograd in April 1917. In July, soldiers began another uprising in Petrograd. Once order was restored, the provisional government ordered Lenin to be arrested, but Lenin fled to Finland. Other leading Bolsheviks escaped or were imprisoned. Later that month, the provisional government appointed Alexander Kerensky as prime minister.

Alexander Feodorovich Kerensky

Alexander Feodorovich Kerensky (*uhl yihk SAHN duhr FEH aw dah RAW vihch kuh REHN skih*) (1881-1970) was an early leader in the Russian Revolution of 1917. He gained fame as a lawyer defending people whom the czarist government had accused of revolutionary activities. After the revolu-

tion that overthrew the czar in March 1917 (February 17 on the old Russian calendar), Kerensky was the only Socialist member of the first provisional government. He became minister of justice, then minister of war, and finally prime minister. His government was well-meaning but indecisive about the popular Bolshevik demand for "peace, bread, and land."

The Communist Bolsheviks overthrew Kerensky's government on Nov. 7, 1917, which was October 25 on the old Russian calendar. Kerensky fled Russia, and he settled in the United States in the 1940's. Kerensky later became a staff member of the Hoover Institution on War, Revolution, and Peace at Stanford University in Stanford, California. He directed a project concerning the Russian Revolution at the institute. Kerensky was born on May 2, 1881, in Simbirsk (now Ul'yanovsk), Russia. He died on June 11, 1970.

Time for action

In September 1917, Lenin wrote the leaders of the Bolsheviks and declared that the time for speechmaking was over. It was time for action. "History will not forgive us if we do not assume power now," Lenin said.

That month, General Lavr Kornilov (*LAV uhr KAWR nee lawv*) (1870-1918), the army commander in chief, made a bid to seize power. As Kornilov advanced on Petrograd, Kerensky released the imprisoned Bolsheviks and allowed them to arm the workers. Kornilov's force broke up before reaching the capital, and the coup attempt ended without violence. With their popularity on the rise, especially among soldiers,

A temporary police force formed by volunteers replaced the czarist police during the Russian Revolution. The volunteers wore white bands with the letters *C. M.*, which stood for *city militia*. In this photograph, volunteers have commandeered an armored car.

the Bolsheviks won a majority in the Petrograd Soviet soon after the "Kornilov affair."

Leon Trotsky, who had escaped in 1907 and gone into exile, had returned to Petrograd in May 1917 and was chosen to head the soviet there in September. Soon after, Lenin returned from Finland.

Trotsky gained control over some government troops. Naval crews also agreed to support the revolt. The Bolsheviks decided to act. On Nov. 7, 1917 (Oct. 25, 1917, on the old calendar), a Bolshevik-led army of workers, soldiers, and sailors took control of key positions in Petrograd. That night, they captured the Winter Palace, which had become the headquarters of Kerensky's provisional government. Kerensky fled Russia, and would settle in the United States in the 1940's. Other cities, including Moscow, soon fell to the Bolsheviks. The struggle for Moscow was more violent than in Petrograd, but by November 15, the Bolsheviks took control.

On Nov. 8, 1917, the All-Russian Congress of Soviets authorized the Bolsheviks to set up a Council of People's Commissars to run the national government. Lenin was made chairman of the council, and so became head of the new Russian state. One of the requests he made in his first appearance before the council was the abolition of private landownership, which was approved, enabling nationalization of all privately owned land. The Bolsheviks altered the name of their Russian Social Democratic Labor Party to the Russian Communist Party. It later became the Communist Party of the Soviet Union. In July 1918, a Soviet constitution went into effect.

In December 1917, the new government established a political police force called the Cheka (*CHEH kuh*). The Cheka helped Lenin enforce his rule by terror. Opponents of the Bolsheviks were imprisoned, murdered, or sent to the Gulag (*goo LAHG* or *GOO lahg*), a system of prison labor

Russian army officers take the oath of allegiance to the October Revolution on Nov. 7, 1917 (Oct. 25, 1917, on the old Russian calendar), in the square of the Winter Palace in Petrograd. Many of the soldiers had previously supported the provisional government of Alexander Kerensky.

Leon Trotsky

Leon Trotsky (1879-1940) was a leader of the Bolshevik revolution in Russia. While the Russian dictator V. I. Lenin lived, Trotsky was the second most powerful man in Russia. After Lenin's death in 1924, Trotsky lost the leadership to Joseph Stalin (1879-1953). Trotsky was later exiled. Until his assassination in Mexico City, Trotsky waged a bitter fight against Stalin from abroad.

Trotsky was born Lev Davidovich Bronstein in Ukraine of well-to-do parents on Nov. 7, 1879. After two years of revolutionary activity as a Social Democrat, he was arrested in 1898. He escaped from Siberian exile in 1902 and went to London, England, where he met Lenin. He returned to Russia to take an active part in the revolution in 1905.

Trotsky was jailed for his leadership in the St. Petersburg Soviet of 1905. But he escaped in 1907. For 10 years, he was a revolutionary writer and editor in western Europe. During World War I, he was expelled from France and Spain and went to New York, where he heard of the czar's downfall in 1917. He returned to Russia. With Lenin, he plotted the seizure of power that brought about a Bolshevik government in November 1917 (October on the old

Leon Trotsky (center) poses with American admirers while he was living in Mexico in April 1940. He was killed there later that month.

Russian calendar). Trotsky became the first Soviet commissar (*KOM uh sahr*), or head of a government department in what became the Soviet Union, of foreign affairs and was soon the commissar of war.

In the civil war of 1918-1920, Trotsky was an efficient organizer of the triumphant Red Army. After Lenin's death, many believed that Trotsky would be the new head of the Soviet government. However, Stalin outsmarted him. Trotsky was expelled from the Communist Party in 1927, and the next year was exiled to Soviet Central Asia. He was deported to Turkey in 1929. He later moved to Norway and then to Mexico.

By 1940, Stalin apparently regretted his "leniency" with Trotsky. His secret police sent an agent to Mexico. Trotsky was stabbed there on Aug. 20, 1940, and died of his wounds the next day. In 1930, Trotsky wrote *My Life: An Attempt at an Autobiography.*

camps where many prisoners died.

Local soviets in towns and cities throughout Russia gave workers control of factories and confiscated the property of large landowners, the Russian Orthodox Church, and anyone who opposed the revolution.

Lenin hardly had time to begin nationalizing industry, banks, and private business, when he found himself battling to stay in power. The Russian Army had fallen apart, the Germans were advancing into Russia, and forces opposing the Bolsheviks were gathering in many parts of the country.

Treaty of Brest-Litovsk

Lenin insisted on ending the war with Germany at any price. He believed that such action was necessary if the Bolsheviks were to stay in power. Trotsky, who was then Russia's commissar of foreign affairs, met with German leaders in Brest-Litovsk to reach an agreement. He sought to end the fighting between Russia and Germany without giving up territory. However, Germany demanded all lands that its armies occupied.

Germany's demands caused a major split within the Russian government. Some Bolsheviks wanted to continue battling, but Lenin insisted on ending the war. Trotsky incorrectly believed that Germany would stop fighting in the war if Russia did. Lenin believed that the agreement with Germany, despite its harsh terms, provided the "breathing space" the Bolsheviks needed if they were to stay in power.

On Dec. 2, 1917, Russia negotiated a cease-fire. The Central Powers invaded Russia in February 1918. They quickly overran large parts of western Russia and increased their already severe demands. On March 3, 1918, Russia and Germany signed the Treaty of Brest-Litovsk. With no option but to sign the treaty, Russia gave up large amounts of its territory, including Bessarabia (now mostly in Moldova), Estonia, Finland, Latvia, Lithuania, Ukraine, part of Belarus, the part of Poland that had been ruled by Russia, and a small piece of territory at the northeastern corner of what is now Turkey. Russia lost many of its factories, about a third of its food-producing land and much of its coal supply, industry, and railroads.

Germany agreed to allow the Russian government to continue ruling the rest of Russia. On March 12, Lenin moved Russia's capital from Petrograd to Moscow, partly so that his government would be farther from German power. The Treaty of Brest-Litovsk was a serious blow to Russia.

The treaty ended the fighting between Russia and the Central Powers and saved the Bolsheviks from further losses in the war. It also gave Lenin's government time to put down revolts in Russia. However, the treaty angered the Allies because it ended the fighting on the Eastern Front and freed German troops for use on the Western Front. In the spring of 1918, Allied troops arrived in Russia to prevent the Germans from seizing war supplies.

The Russian government revoked the treaty in November 1918, following Germany's defeat in World War I. The Russian Communist forces then moved to occupy much of the territory that had been lost as a result of the treaty.

Barely a month after the October Revolution, the counterrevolutionaries known as the Whites began organizing resistance. Trotsky organized the Red Army, created by Lenin, to fight the counterrevolutionaries as well as foreign intervention. The Red (Communist) Russians, aided by the peasantry, fought a bloody civil war with the Whites for nearly three years. The Whites received support from several other countries, including Canada, France, Japan, the United Kingdom, and

Red Army

The Red Army was the national army of Russia and the Soviet Union from 1918 to 1946. Following the Russian Revolution of 1917, in January 1918, the Bolsheviks formed the Red Army—officially called the Workers' and Peasants' Red Army. The army was called "Red" because of the red flag and red star that symbolized Communism. The Red Army was created from the Red Guards, a workers' militia that defended the Communist Party. Initially, the Red Army was a volunteer force led by Leon Trotsky, a Bolshevik leader and *commissar* (minister) of war.

From 1918 to 1920, Communists and anti-Communists fought a civil war for control of Russia. During this time, the Red Army grew from about 300,000 soldiers to around 5 million. In the civil war, the Red Army defeated the anti-Communist "Whites," who were supported by troops from several other countries, including Canada, France, Japan, the United Kingdom, and the United States. In 1920, the Red Army lost a brief war with Poland. In 1922, the Communist government joined Russia with three other territories to create the Soviet Union.

By 1925, the Red Army had decreased in size to roughly 500,000 troops. It also underwent a reform program. Mikhail Tukhachevsky (*mih kah EEL too kah CHEHV skee*) (1893-1937), one of the highest-ranking officers in the Red Army, helped create large tank, mechanized, and airborne units. In 1937, Tukhachevsky was murdered in one of the purges ordered by Soviet dictator Joseph Stalin that sought to eliminate anyone who might threaten Stalin's power. By 1941, Stalin had expanded the Red Army to about 5 million soldiers. He also equipped the Army

Red Army soldiers advance near Moscow in January 1942, during World War II. The Red Army turned back a German attack just 20 miles (32 kilometers) from the Soviet capital.

with new tanks and warplanes.

In August 1939, just before the start of World War II (1939-1945), the Soviet Union and Germany signed a *nonaggression pact.* The pact was an agreement that neither nation would attack the other. Stalin then lowered Soviet defenses. However, in June 1941, Germany launched a surprise attack on the Soviet Union, and the Red Army suffered massive losses. Despite this disaster and the ongoing war, the Red Army grew into a modern force of over 9 million troops. The army stopped major German offensives at Moscow in 1941, Stalingrad (now Volgograd) in 1942, and Kursk in 1943. The Germans were driven back and eventually surrendered in May 1945. In 1946, the Red Army was renamed the Soviet Army.

the United States. However, the Whites were unable to organize effectively. Foreign-led resistance to the government continued in eastern Siberia for almost two years. By 1920, the Communists had won and the revolution was complete.

On March 3, 1918, the Bolshevik government of Russia signed a treaty with the Central Powers (Germany, Austria-Hungary, Bulgaria, and the Ottoman Empire) at Brest-Litovsk (now Brest, Belarus). Russia gave up large amounts of its territory, including Bessarabia (now mostly in Moldova), Estonia, Finland, Latvia, Lithuania, Ukraine, part of Belarus, the part of Poland that had been ruled by Russia, and a small piece of territory at the northeastern corner of what is now Turkey.

Joseph Stalin established comprehensive economic plans for Russia that included provisions to combine small peasant farms into collective farms. He transferred farm equipment and livestock to the government.

CHAPTER SIX

Communist Russia after the civil war

As Communist Russia transitioned after the civil war, Lenin found a need to revive the economy because a lack of business activity created unrest.

After the civil war, Lenin took extreme measures to keep control of his weakened country. In March 1921, he introduced a program called the New Economic Policy (NEP). The NEP replaced many of the socialist measures started at the beginning of his rule. Small businesses were permitted to resume limited operations. Free retail trade was allowed again. Foreign businesses were invited to invest in Russia. Peasants could sell food to private customers. Food supplies sent by the American Relief Administration saved hundreds of thousands of starving Russians.

The NEP called for Communists to cooperate with certain groups that were considered enemies of Communism. These included shopkeepers, peasants, engineers, scholars, and army officers.

Communist Russia gradually transformed itself into the Soviet Union after regaining territory lost through the Brest-Litovsk Treaty and during the civil war. Russia also suppressed nationalist movements in central Asia and what is now Belarus. In 1922, the Russian Communist government formed the Union of Soviet Socialist Republics, or Soviet Union.

At first, many foreign nations refused to recognize the new Soviet government. The United Kingdom recognized the Soviet Union in 1924, followed by the United States in 1933.

Death of Lenin; rise of Stalin

In April 1922, Lenin appointed Joseph Stalin as general secretary of the Communist Party. Lenin soon began harboring serious doubts about Stalin and planned to remove him as party secretary. But on March 9, 1923, Lenin had a third stroke within a year and lost his power to speak clearly, keeping him from appointing a new party secretary. Stalin gained control of the Soviet Union after Lenin died of a brain hemorrhage on Jan. 21, 1924.

Farmers eat lunch in the fields during harvesting time on a collective farm in the village of Vilshanka, in the Kiev region's Shashkovsky district.

By the time Lenin died, the Soviet Union had become a one-party state. All non-Communist political parties had been banned, and all public organizations—such as professional associations and labor unions—had become tools of the Communists.

Stalin ruled with an iron hand from 1929 until he died in 1953. The Soviet Union's economy and influence abroad grew rapidly—but at a great cost in human life and personal freedom at home.

Stalin established a centrally planned economy in the Soviet Union. In 1928, he began the *five-year plans,* which were comprehensive economic plans for the country. The government began eliminating private businesses. Production of industrial machinery and farm equipment became more important, while production of clothing and household goods was neglected. The first plan included *provisions* (laws) that combined small peasant farms into *collective farms,* large farms owned and controlled by the government. Stalin transferred farm equipment and livestock to the government.

In the early 1930's, Stalin ordered millions of peasants murdered or exiled when they resisted giving their land to collective farms. Farmers who resisted Stalin's order destroyed about half of the U.S.S.R.'s livestock and much of its produce. The destruction of livestock and grain caused widespread starvation. The economy moved forward, but at the cost of millions of lives.

Stalin also turned over many industries to the secret police, who forced prisoners to work in them. Fear spread through the U.S.S.R. as neighbors were ordered to spy on one another. The Soviet government broke up families, urging children to inform on their parents to the police.

Millions of Soviets opposed Stalin's policies during the 1930's. To crush this opposition, Stalin began a program of terror called the Great Purge.

Joseph Stalin

Joseph Stalin (*STAH lihn*) (1879-1953) was dictator of the Soviet Union from 1929 until 1953. He rose from bitter poverty to become ruler of a country that covered about a sixth of the world's land area.

Stalin was born on Dec. 21, 1879, in Gori, a town near Tbilisi in Georgia, a mountainous area in what was the southwestern part of the Russian empire. His real name was Iosif Vissarionovich Djugashvili. In 1913, he adopted the name *Stalin* from a Russian word that means *man of steel*.

Stalin ruled by terror during most of his years as dictator. He allowed no one to oppose his decisions. Stalin executed or jailed most of those who had helped him rise to power because he feared they might threaten his rule.

Stalin also was responsible for the deaths of millions of Soviet peasants who opposed his program of *collective agriculture* (government control of farms). Under Stalin, the Soviet Union operated a worldwide network of Communist parties. By the time he died, Communism had spread to 11 other countries. His style of government became known as *Stalinism* and continued to influence many governments.

The Soviet people had cause to hate Stalin, and much of the

world feared him. But he changed the Soviet Union from an undeveloped country into one of the world's great industrial and military powers. In World War II, the Soviet Union was an ally of the United States and the United Kingdom against Germany. But Stalin sharply opposed and, on occasion, betrayed his allies. The last years that Stalin ruled the Soviet Union were marked by the Cold War, in which many non-Communist nations banded together to halt the spread of Communism.

Stalin could not take criticism, and he never forgave an opponent. Few dictators have demanded such terrible sacrifices from their own people. After Stalin became dictator, he had Soviet histories rewritten to make his role in past events appear far greater than it really was. In 1938, he helped write an official history of the Communist Party. Stalin had not played a leading part in the revolution of November 1917 (October by the old Russian calendar), which brought Communism to Russia. V. I. Lenin led this revolution, which is known as the October Revolution, and set up the world's first Communist government. But in his history, Stalin pictured himself as Lenin's chief assistant in the revolution.

Stalin died in 1953. He was honored by having his body placed beside that of Lenin in a huge tomb in Red Square in Moscow. In 1956, Nikita S. Khrushchev strongly criticized Stalin for his terrible crimes against loyal Communists. Later, in 1961, the government renamed many cities, towns, and factories that had been named for Stalin. Stalin's body was taken from the tomb and buried in a simple grave nearby.

Communists suspected of opposing Stalin or his policies were executed or imprisoned. Stalin ordered many of his earlier Communist associates arrested or put to death. Stalin started eliminating most of the old Bolsheviks associated with Lenin in 1935. During the next few years, he killed anyone who might have threatened his power. Numerous party officials were labeled "enemies of the people" and forced to confess imaginary crimes. The secret police assisted in the purges, in which army officers and citizens from all walks of life were imprisoned, sent to labor camps, or killed. The peak of mass terror came between 1936 and 1938.

Stalin achieved his purpose. When he decided to cooperate with the German Nazi dictator Adolf Hitler (1889-1945) in 1939, there was no one left to oppose his policies. Even when the Soviet Union later suffered terrible military defeats from Hitler's army, no political opposition to Stalin was possible.

During World War II, political repression in the Soviet Union eased somewhat. The Soviet people rallied to defend their country from the invading Nazis. But after the war ended, Stalin's secret police returned to using terror to maintain strict control over the people.

Lavrenti Pavlovich Beria (*lav REHN tee pah VLAW vihch BEHR ee u*) (1899-1953), chief of the secret police, became a leading figure in Stalin's government. Police control grew tighter. The bloody purges went on, but in secret. No one was safe. Even Politburo (*puh LIHT byur oh* or *POL iht byoor oh*) members and Communist Party leaders were purged and shot in 1949 and 1950. Anti-Semitism, prejudice against Jews, which had been encouraged by Stalin during the 1930's, was now practiced throughout the country.

During the 1930's, Stalin attempted to make Russian culture and the Russian language dominant throughout the U.S.S.R. The minority

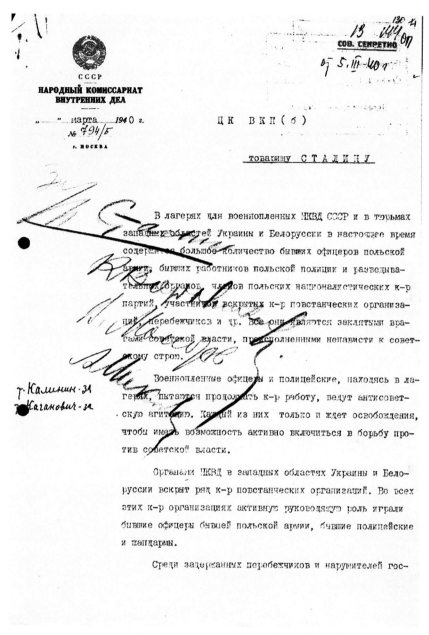

СССР

НАРОДНЫЙ КОМИССАРИАТ ВНУТРЕННИХ ДЕЛ

" " марта 1940 г.

№ 794/Б

г. МОСКВА

СОВ. СЕКРЕТНО

Ц К   В К П (б)

товарищу С Т А Л И Н У

В лагерях для военнопленных НКВД СССР и в тюрьмах западных областей Украины и Белоруссии в настоящее время содержится большое количество бывших офицеров польской армии, бывших работников польской полиции и разведывательных органов, членов польских националистических к-р партий, участников вскрытых к-р повстанческих организаций, перебежчиков и пр. Все они являются заклятыми врагами советской власти, преисполненными ненависти к советскому строю.

Военнопленные офицеры и полицейские, находясь в лагерях, пытаются продолжать к-р работу, ведут антисоветскую агитацию. Каждый из них только и ждет освобождения, чтобы иметь возможность активно включиться в борьбу против советской власти.

Органами НКВД в западных областях Украины и Белоруссии вскрыт ряд к-р повстанческих организаций. Во всех этих к-р организациях активную руководящую роль играли бывшие офицеры бывшей польской армии, бывшие полицейские и жандармы.

Среди задержанных перебежчиков и нарушителей гос-

т. Калинин - за

т. Каганович - за

Communists suspected of opposing Joseph Stalin or his policies were executed or imprisoned. The top secret document above is an accepted proposal issued in March 1940 to execute former Polish army and police officers in NKVD prisons and prisoner of war camps. NKVD was the secret police force of Communist Russia and the Soviet Union from 1934 to 1943.

The Politburo

The Politburo (*puh LIHT byur oh* or *POL iht byoor oh*) was the political bureau of the Central Committee that controlled the Communist Party of the Soviet Union from 1919 to 1991. Before 1990, the Politburo included the most powerful members of the party, and all-important decisions in the Soviet government needed the Politburo's approval. But in 1990, the Politburo's power was greatly reduced when its role was limited to the development of party policy. In August 1991, several Communist officials failed in an attempt to overthrow Soviet President Mikhail Gorbachev (*mih kah EEL gawr buh CHAWF*) and take control of the government. After the attempt, the Soviet parliament suspended all Communist Party activities, including those of the Politburo. In December 1991, the Soviet Union broke up into a number of independent states.

V. I. Lenin, the country's first leader, set up the Politburo in 1919. In 1952, the Politburo became the Presidium (*prih SIHD ee uhm*) of the Central Committee. The Presidium was the chief executive and policy-making body of the Soviet Communist Party. In 1966, the Presidium was renamed the Politburo. Lenin dominated the Politburo until his death in 1924. Joseph Stalin later gained

Joseph Stalin (fourth from right) gained control of the Politiburo and replaced his adversaries with hand-picked associates.

control of it and replaced his adversaries with hand-picked associates. After Stalin's death in 1953, Nikita Khrushchev handled the Presidium the same way.

The first Politburo had five members. But for many years, the Politburo usually had from 10 to 15 full members and from 7 to 10 *candidate* (nonvoting) members. In 1990, its membership was set at 24 full members. The name *Politburo* also is used for similar groups in other Communist countries.

Shortly after Joseph Stalin died in 1953, Nikita S. Khrushchev (front row, second from left) became head of the Soviet Communist Party. In 1958, Khrushchev also became the head of the Soviet government. He strongly criticized Stalin for his rule by terror. Khrushchev relaxed political control over writers, artists, and scholars. He also introduced reforms designed to improve the productivity and efficiency of the economy. He is shown at a session of the Supreme Soviet in Moscow in 1961.

nationalities in the Soviet Union were subject to increasingly strict control by the government. In 1939, the Soviet Union seized a large part of Poland. In 1940, Soviet troops invaded the Baltic countries—Estonia, Latvia, and Lithuania. Stalin tried to destroy the middle classes in these countries. He set up Communist governments and joined the countries to the Soviet Union.

Khrushchev, Brezhnev, and Gorbachev

Shortly after Stalin died in 1953, Nikita S. Khrushchev (*nih KEE tuh KROOSH chehf*) (1894-1971) became head of the Soviet Communist Party. In 1958, Khrushchev also became the head of the Soviet government. He strongly criticized Stalin for his rule by terror. Khrushchev relaxed political control over writers, artists, and scholars. He also introduced reforms designed to improve the productivity and efficiency of the economy. But Khrushchev's reforms resulted in only slow gains.

In 1964, Communist Party officials forced Khrushchev to retire.

Leonid I. Brezhnev (*LAY oh nihd BREHZH nyehf*) (1906-1982) replaced Khrushchev as head of the Communist Party. Brezhnev reestablished many of Stalin's rigid cultural and economic policies but did not return to rule by terror.

After Brezhnev's death in 1982, two other leaders briefly headed the government and the party. But no major changes were enacted until Mikhail S. Gorbachev (1931-   ) became head of the country in 1985.

The Communist system finally ended in Russia in 1991, two years after it had collapsed in the East European countries. The Soviet Union itself also broke up.

Leonid I. Brezhnev (right) replaced Nikita S. Khrushchev as head of the Communist Party. He met with U.S. President Jimmy Carter at the SALT II treaty conference in Vienna, Austria, in 1979. The treaty was negotiated to limit the use of nuclear weapons by the United States and the Soviet Union.

A struggling Soviet economy

The Soviet Union struggled economically from the 1970's onward, as many Communist nations did during that time. With that came a dissatisfied middle class, and disappointment with the Communist political system among key members of the political elite. By the late 1980's, most Communist countries had experienced long periods of little or no economic growth. Centralized planning proved to be inefficient, and it hindered the development of new technologies. As a result, most Communist countries could not compete economically with Japan and the industrial powers of the West. Economic reforms introduced by Gorbachev included lifting the ban on private businesses run by families and individuals, and modifications in the central planning system. Still, the end of Communism would be a shock to the system for Russians as they adjusted to having free enterprise for the first time in 74 years.

While numerous countries adopted Communist regimes during the rise of the Soviet Union, few remained after the fall of the U.S.S.R. By 1992, Communists held a monopoly on power in only a few countries, including China, Cuba, Laos, North Korea, and Vietnam. But the governments of China and Vietnam were introducing economic reforms.

Russia maintained Communist rule for 74 years. Strong central government was a signature part of it, as well as a centrally planned economy and military strength. Rule by terror only remained a hallmark until Stalin died. While numerous countries adopted Communist regimes during the era of Communist Russia, it did not occur in the internationally coordinated way Lenin envisioned.

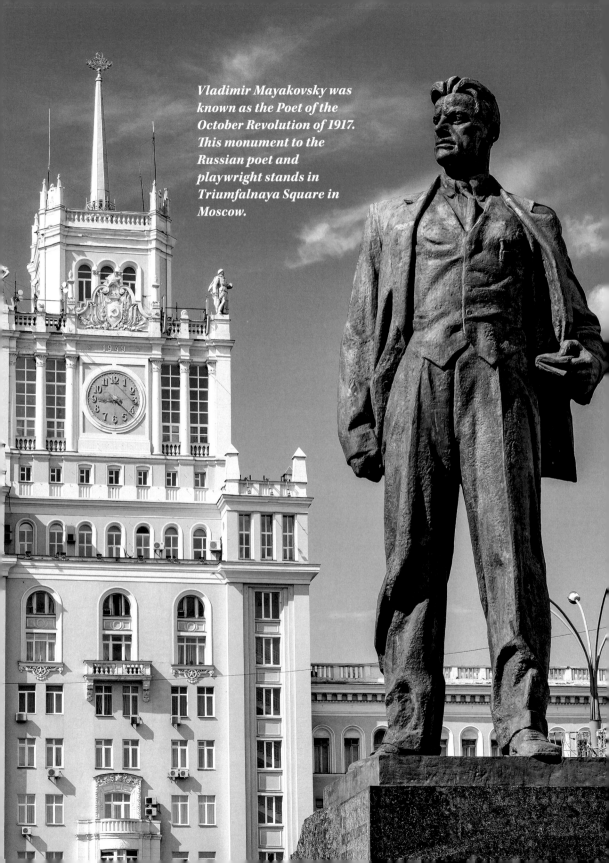

Vladimir Mayakovsky was known as the Poet of the October Revolution of 1917. This monument to the Russian poet and playwright stands in Triumfalnaya Square in Moscow.

CHAPTER SEVEN

Literature of the revolution

T he Russian Revolution of 1917 marked the beginning of a new era in Russian literature. For a few years, many writers engaged in creative experimentation. Then, the new Communist government tightened censorship, which had also existed under the czars. Many writers who opposed the Communist government left the country or were imprisoned or executed. Those who remained had to serve the interests of the state or stop writing.

One of the writers who stayed in the country was the poet and playwright Vladimir Mayakovsky (*VLAD uh mihr* or *vlah DEE mihr muh yih KAWF skee*) (1893-1930). He became one of the great poets of the 1900's. Mayakovsky was known as the Poet of the October Revolution of 1917, At the age of 14, Mayakovsky joined what became the Bolshevik wing of the Communist Party. He was imprisoned for political activities in 1909 and began writing poetry while in prison. Upon his release after serving 11 months, he joined a group that shared his revolutionary attitude toward Russia's social order and cultural traditions and had an equally radical program in the arts. Mayakovsky later devoted himself to pro-Soviet propaganda.

Another notable Russian writer from the early period of Soviet Russian literature was the short-story writer Isaak Babel (1894-1938?). He fought on the side of the Bolsheviks during the Russian civil war. His experiences provided material for *Konarmia* (1926), a collection of short stories called *Red Cavalry* in the English translation. He wrote these stories in a

Vladimir Mayakovsky

Vladimir Mayakovsky (*VLAD uh mihr* or *vlah DEE mihr muh yih KAWF skee*) (1893-1930), a Russian poet and playwright, was one of the great poets of the 1900's. He became known as the Poet of the October Revolution of 1917, the revolution that established the Communist Soviet government in Russia.

Vladimir Vladimirovich Mayakovsky was born in the Georgian city of Bagdadi on July 19 (July 7 on the Russian calendar then in use), 1893. At the age of 14, Mayakovsky joined what became the Bolshevik wing of the Communist Party. He was imprisoned for political activities in 1909 and began writing poetry while in prison. Upon his release after serving 11 months, he entered the Moscow Art School to study painting. There, he joined a group that shared his revolutionary attitude toward Russia's social order and cultural traditions and had an equally radical program in the arts.

Mayakovsky's strikingly unconventional love poems "The Cloud in Trousers" (1914-1915) and "The Backbone Flute" (1916) achieved popular success. They treated romantic love in terms of revolutionary street violence and pain, all in jarring, marchlike rhythms.

Mayakovsky soon devoted himself to pro-Soviet propaganda. In 1924, he wrote a long elegy on the death of the revolutionary leader V. I. Lenin. In the mid-1920's, Mayakovsky traveled to western Europe and Latin America as a cultural ambassador. During this period, he wrote the narrative poem "Good" (1925), an example of his praise of his Soviet homeland. "The Brooklyn Bridge" (1925) is an odelike poem that shows the futuristic worship of technology and urban life.

In the late 1920's, Mayakovsky came to regret having sacrificed his talent on what he saw as propaganda. He wrote two satirical plays, *The Bedbug* (1929) and *The Bathhouse* (1930), which exposed the bureaucracy and artistic narrow-mindedness of Soviet life. Both plays angered Soviet authorities. Suffering from depression brought on by personal and artistic frustration, Mayakovsky died by suicide on April 14, 1930.

striking ornamental prose. Babel, who was born in Odessa, Russia, wrote another collection, *Odessa Tales* (1927), which depicts the life of Odessa Jews. Babel disappeared in 1938. Soviet police apparently arrested and executed him.

Alexei Tolstoy (*TOL stoy* or *TOHL stoy*) (1882-1945) was another Russian novelist and playwright from this period. His most important novel is the three-part *Road to Calvary* (1921, 1927, 1941). This epic tale describes the tragedies of Russian life during World War I and deals with the Bolshevik

Russian short-story writer Isaak Babel fought on the side of the Bolsheviks during the Russian civil war. His experiences provided material for *Konarmia* (1926), a collection of short stories called *Red Cavalry* in the English translation.

Revolution of 1917 and the ensuing Russian civil war. The novel recounts the effects of these events on a group of intellectuals.

One group of Russian artists, writers, and intellectuals who fled Russia following the October Revolution of 1917 included the novelists Vladimir Nabokov (*VLAH duh meer NAH boh kawf*) (1899-1977) and Maxim Gorki (*mahk SEEM GAWR kee*) (1868-1936), the writer Nina Berberova (1901-1993), and her first husband, the poet Vladislav Khodasevich.

Nabokov fled with his family to Western Europe in 1919 after the Bolshevik revolution. From 1922 to 1940, he lived in Berlin and Paris

Maxim Gorki

Maxim Gorki (*mahk SEEM GAWR kee*) (1868-1936) was a Russian novelist, playwright, and short-story writer. He vividly portrayed the poverty of peasants and workers, as well as the decay and narrow-mindedness of the middle class before the Communist Revolution of 1917. *The Lower Depths* (1902), Gorki's most popular play, describes the miserable lives of the inhabitants of a cheap boarding house. His most famous novel, *The Mother* (1907), tells the story of an old peasant woman who is converted to the revolutionary cause.

Gorki was born in March 1868 in Nizhniy Novgorod, later renamed Gorki in his honor. His real name was Alexey Maximovich Peshkov. He took the pen name *Gorki,* a Russian word meaning *bitter,* to express his criticism of the Russian political and social order. Gorki had only a few months of schooling and was largely self-educated. He roamed throughout Russia, going from job to job. He described his wanderings in his three-volume autobiography—*Childhood* (1913), *In the World* (1916), and *My Universities* (1923). In the early 1930's, he helped institute the Soviet doctrine of literature and art called *Socialist Realism.*

Gorki died on June 14, 1936, while undergoing medical treatment. The Soviet authorities accused his doctors of poisoning him. But the true circumstances of his death remain unknown.

among other Russians who had left their country because of the revolution. Nabokov wrote his novels in Russian, and most were later translated into English. He began writing in English after moving to the United States in 1940.

Gorki vividly portrayed the poverty of peasants and workers, as well as the decay and narrow-mindedness of the middle class before the revolution of 1917. His most famous novel, *The Mother* (1907), tells the story of an old peasant woman who is converted to the revolutionary cause. In the 1930's, he helped institute the Socialist Realism movement. For much of his life, Gorki was exiled from Russia and later the Soviet Union.

Berberova gained recognition late in her life. In 1922, she went first to Berlin and then, in 1925, to Paris, where she lived for 25 years. In 1950, Berberova moved to the United States. She wrote poems, novels, and short stories as well as biography, memoirs, criticism, and reviews. Berberova felt that life was not entirely a matter of free will or conscious choice and that, sometimes, forces outside human control shaped lives. Her fiction often underlines the difference between a life of endurance and bare survival and one of self-knowledge and action.

Russian literature after the revolution

Following the revolution, publishing houses closed and book production and sales dropped as a civil war devastated the economy. Newspapers and magazines became political tools of the Communist Party. The government encouraged the development of a proletarian literature to express the interests of Russian workers and peasants.

Russian literature rebounded during the 1920's. The government restored some literary freedom, reopened publishing houses, and permitted literary criticism to resume. Many new young poets and novel-

Newspapers and magazines became political tools of the Communist Party. These publications circulated throughout many parts of the world. In this photograph, taken in 1937, a newsstand in New York City displays several Communist propaganda magazines.

The period of industrial literature began in 1928 with the Soviet Union's first five-year plan. Factory and production novels began to appear in the Soviet Union, describing the building of a factory or the organization of collective farms. This photograph shows a Soviet garment factory in 1967.

ists in the Soviet Union at this time became known as *fellow travelers* (people willing to cooperate with the Soviet regime though they did not actively support it).

The period of industrial literature began in 1928 with the Soviet Union's first five-year plan. This program aimed, in part, to build up Soviet industry. Writers were expected to produce works dealing with economic problems. Factory and production novels began to appear in the Soviet Union, describing the building of a factory or the organization of collective farms.

Socialist Realism and censorship

The period of Socialist Realism started in the early 1930's. The government of Joseph Stalin believed that literature was important. It banned private literary associations and established a Union of Soviet Writers. All professional writers were required to join the union, which endorsed the new doctrine of Socialist Realism. According to this doctrine, the main purpose of literature is to portray the building of a socialist society. A *socialist society* is one that emphasizes public or community ownership of all property that produces goods and services. The union ordered Soviet authors to produce optimistic works that were easy to understand and similar to the style of Gorki and the great Russian novelist Leo Tolstoy (1828-1910).

Censorship eliminated undesirable material from manuscripts, and writers soon learned to censor themselves. Writers who ignored the doctrine were expelled from the union. This meant the end of their careers, and some writers were imprisoned or even killed.

Historical literature became more common during the 1930's and early 1940's. The scholar Yuri Tynyanov wrote novels set in the 1800's based on his research on literary history. One of the finest works about the revolution and the civil war was *The Quiet Don* (1928-1940) by Mikhail Sholokhov (*mih kah EEL SHAW lo kawf*) (1905-1984). This long epic novel tells the story of a young Cossack whose happiness is destroyed by the tragedy of war. Sholokhov received the Nobel Prize for literature in 1965.

During the war against Germany from 1941 to 1945, the Soviet government gave writers greater freedom, hoping to build the nation's morale. Themes of individual suffering and death dominated this period. Not long after the war ended, the government reestablished strict controls over literature. For most of the time from 1930 to 1953, writers did their best work "for the desk drawer" and only published it after Stalin's death in

Mikhail Sholokhov

Mikhail Sholokhov *(mih kah EEL SHAW lo kawf)* (1905-1984), a Soviet writer, received the Nobel Prize in literature in 1965. Mikhail Alexandrovich Sholokhov was born on May 24, 1905, in Veshenskaya, a Cossack village in southwestern Russia. He won fame for novels and stories describing the life and people of his native region. His best-known work is the four-volume historical novel *The Quiet Don* (1928-1940). This epic story describes the effects of the Russian Revolution of 1917, and of the civil war that followed, on the lives of the Don Cossacks. Don Cossacks are Cossacks who settled along the middle and lower Don River in southwestern Russia. Sholokhov also wrote *Virgin Soil Upturned* (1932, 1955-1960), a two-volume novel about the problems of Don Cossacks living on collective farms. His early works include the short-story collections *Tales of the Don* (1925) and *The Azure Steppe* (1926). He died on Feb. 21, 1984.

1953. In the early 1950's, some of the most prominent Jewish writers in the Soviet Union were arrested and many of them were killed, especially those who wrote and published in Yiddish.

Stalin's death was followed by a period of relaxed restrictions in Soviet life and literature. This change became known as *The Thaw*, from the title of a short novel by Soviet writer Ilya Ehrenburg published in 1954.

Soviet writer Ilya Ehrenburg wrote the short novel *The Thaw* (1954). In contrast to the policy of describing Soviet life as happy and optimistic, Ehrenburg wrote about frustrated, lonely people. In this photograph, Ehrenburg is shown giving a speech in 1946.

Anna Akhmatova

Anna Akhmatova (*ahk MAH tuh vuh*) (1889-1966) was the pen name of Anna Andreyevna Gorenko, one of the most important woman poets in Russian literature. Akhmatova was noted for her skill with language and her emotional and artistic honesty. Akhmatova's best work demonstrates her ability to describe the feelings experienced by all human beings, especially love.

Akhmatova was born on June 23 (June 11 on the Russian calendar then in use), 1889, at Bolshoy Fontan, near the Black Sea port of Odessa, Russia (now in Ukraine). While she was still a child, her father, a retired naval officer, moved the family to the St. Petersburg area. There, Anna attended a *gymnasium* (junior and high school). She completed her gymnasium education in Kiev and briefly studied law there.

Akhmatova began writing poetry at the age of 11. When she was 22, she joined a group of Russian poets in St. Petersburg called the Acmeists and soon became one of its leading figures. The group opposed the vague and abstract poetry of the Russian Symbolist poets of the time. Instead, the Acmeists tried to write clear, simple, compact, and well-crafted poems about real people and real feelings.

Akhmatova's earliest poems are outstanding examples of the Acmeist style. The poems are brief, highly personal lyrics, written in everyday language. Most of the verses deal with frustrated love. Her early collections include *Evening* (1912), *Rosary* (1914), *The White Flock* (1917), and *Anno Domini MCMXXI* (1922).

The Russian Revolution of 1917 led to the establishment of the Soviet Union in 1922, eventually led by dictator Joseph Stalin. Soviet critics condemned Akhmatova's poetry for its emphasis on love and God, which did not follow the government political guidelines on literature. In 1925, a Communist Party resolution banned her poetry. Akhmatova did not publish any poetry from 1923 to 1940.

After the German invasion of Russia in 1941, Akhmatova wrote and recited some war-inspired poems and began to have her work published. In 1946, the government again condemned her poetry. She was expelled from the Union of Soviet Writers, a union of professional writers formed by the Communist Party.

Following the death of Stalin in 1953, Akhmatova's work slowly came back into favor. In 1958, a book of her poems was published. Starting in the early 1960's, her works became internationally known through translation. One of Akhmatova's finest later works is *Requiem* (written 1935-1940 and first published in 1963). This series of poems depicts the sufferings of the Russian people under Stalin's harsh rule. Another major work is *Poem Without a Hero* (written 1940-1962 and published in its final form in the 1970's). This complex piece is woven around the central tragedy of a young poet's suicide. Akhmatova died on March 5, 1966. Her reputation has continued to grow after her death.

Pravda (Truth) was the official newspaper of the Communist Party of the Soviet Union until the Communists lost control of the Soviet government in 1991. Pravda was established in 1912, in St. Petersburg, where V. I. Lenin was one of its chief contributors. This photograph shows a worker in the *Pravda* print shop in 1959.

Censorship in the Soviet Union prevented many works from being published, though typewritten or *mimeographed* copies of some of the manuscripts circulated secretly. Mimeograph machines made duplicate copies from a stencil. This type of self-publishing became known as *samizdat* (*sahm ihz DAHT*). Some Soviet writers published works abroad that had not been officially published in their own country.

From 1970 to 1991, political restrictions made publishing difficult in the Soviet Union. But many writers continued to resist or stretch the

In the mid-1980's, Soviet leader Mikhail Gorbachev introduced a policy of *glasnost*, meaning openness, that relaxed censorship and led to freer public expression of information and opinion.

rules of Socialist Realism. In the mid-1980's, Soviet leader Mikhail Gorbachev introduced a policy of *glasnost* (*GLAHS nawst*), meaning openness, that relaxed censorship and led to freer public expression of information and opinion. The Soviet Union began publishing uncensored works of such important Soviet writers as Anna Akhmatova (*ahk MAH tuh vuh*) (1889-1966), Mikhail Bulgakov (1891-1940), and Boris Pasternak (*PAS tuhr nak*) (1890-1960).

The Gorbachev period and the following years of political transition in Russia saw the publication of numerous translations from foreign languages and also of works by formerly suppressed writers. The era of Soviet literature ended in 1991, when the Soviet Union broke up into many independent countries.

Boris Pasternak

Boris Pasternak (*PAS tuhr nak*) (1890-1960) was a Russian poet and fiction writer. In the West, he is best known for his novel *Dr. Zhivago* (1957). Pasternak was awarded the Nobel Prize for literature in 1958. He accepted the award but then rejected it under pressure from the Soviet government.

Authorities banned *Dr. Zhivago* in the Soviet Union. The novel was first published in Italy and then was translated into English and many other languages. Zhivago, a Russian physician, experiences the suffering and disorder of his country's revolutionary period. He cannot accept Communist rule and tries to find happiness in love and in the beauty of nature. The novel contains much autobiographical material. Zhivago is also a poet and his beautiful poems are part of the book.

Boris Leonidovich Pasternak was born on Feb. 10, 1890, in Moscow. He showed great promise in musical composition and philosophy before turning to poetry. His third book of poems, *My Sister Life* (1922), established his reputation as a major Russian poet. For Russians, his greatness as a poet is paramount.

Pasternak's poems supported the Russian revolutions of

EUROPEAN POETRY CLASSICS

BORIS PASTERNAK

My Sister—Life

Translated from the Russian by Mark Rudman with Bohdan Boychuk

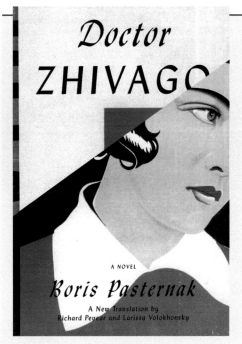

Doctor ZHIVAGO

A NOVEL

Boris Pasternak

A New Translation by
Richard Pevear and Larissa Volokhonsky

Boris Pasternak's third book of poems, *My Sister Life* (1922) (above left) established his reputation as a major Russian poet. He was awarded the Nobel Prize for literature in 1958 for *Dr. Zhivago* (1957) (above right). The book's title character, a Russian physician, experiences the suffering and disorder of his country's revolutionary period.

1905 and 1917, but he did not accept many of the strict doctrines of the Communist Party. During the 1930's and 1940's, the Soviet government prohibited the publication of most of Pasternak's writing. He earned a living by translating poems and plays by foreign writers. In 1957, the Soviet Writers Union expelled Pasternak, which meant that his works could not be published in the Soviet Union. He died on May 30, 1960. The union reinstated him in 1987, almost 27 years after his death. In 1988, *Dr. Zhivago* was first published in the Soviet Union.

INDEX

FIND OUT MORE!

D'Agostino, Anthony. *The Russian Revolution, 1917-1945.* Greenwood, 2010.

Engelstein, Laura. *Russia in Flames: War, Revolution, Civil War, 1914 - 1921.* Oxford, 2018.

Kalic, Sean N., and Brown, G. M., eds. *Russian Revolution of 1917: The Essential Reference Guide.* ABC-CLIO, 2017.

Miéville, China. *October: The Story of the Russian Revolution.* Verso, 2017.

ACKNOWLEDGMENTS

Cover:	© Everett Historical/ Shutterstock; © Aleksandr Kurganov, Shutterstock	**38-39**	*Marx and Engels at the Neue Rheinische Zeitung,* by E.N. Sapiro; International Institute of Social History	**108**	© Viacheslav Lopatin, Shutterstock
4	© Everett Historical/ Shutterstock	**41**	Public Domain	**110**	Public Domain
6	*Ivan the Terrible shows his treasures to the English ambassador Horsey* (1875), oil on canvas by Alexander Litovchenko; Russian Museum	**43**	© Everett Historical/ Shutterstock	**112-113**	Public Domain; Library of Congress
		45	Public Domain	**115**	© Alfred Eisenstaedt, The LIFE Picture Collection/ Getty Images
		46	WORLD BOOK map		
		48	© Everett Historical/ Shutterstock	**116**	Yury Artamonov, RIA Novosti archive (licensed under CC-BY-SA 3.0)
11	Public Domain	**51**	Public Domain	**118-119**	© Bettmann/Getty Images; © Marie Hansen, The LIFE Picture Collection/Getty Images
12	WORLD BOOK map	**53**	WORLD BOOK map		
13	*Tsar Ivan The Terrible* (1897), oil on canvas by Viktor Vasnetsov; Tretyakov Gallery (Moscow)	**55**	© Everett Historical/ Shutterstock		
		57-59	Library of Congress	**121**	© TASS/Getty Images
		61-62	© Everett Historical/ Shutterstock	**122-123**	A. Cheprunov, RIA Novosti archive (licensed under CC-BY-SA 3.0); Yuryi Abramochkin, RIA Novosti archive (licensed under CC-BY-SA 3.0)
15	WORLD BOOK map	**65-69**	Public Domain		
17	Public Domain	**72-73**	© Thinkstock		
18-19	*Yermak's conquest of Siberia* (1895), oil on canvas by Vasiliy Surikov; Russian Museum	**76-77**	© Topical Press Agency/ Getty Images; © Marco Rubino, Shutterstock		
				124	© ITAR-TASS/Alamy Images
21	© Everett Historical/ Shutterstock	**78-81**	Public Domain		
24	*Peter I the Great* (1838), oil on canvas by Paul Delaroche; Kunsthalle Hamburg	**82-85**	© Everett Historical/ Shutterstock		
		86-87	Public Domain; National Archives		
27	Public Domain	**91**	Oleg Ignatovich, RIA Novosti archive (licensed under CC-BY-SA 3.0)		
29	*Portrait of Catherine II* (1782), oil on canvas by Dmitry Levitzky; Tretyakov Gallery (Moscow)	**92-93**	© Everett Historical/ Shutterstock		
		94	© Everett Historical/ Shutterstock		
		96	© Bettmann/Getty Images		
30-32	© Everett Historical/ Shutterstock	**98**	Public Domain		
35	Public Domain	**101**	Public Domain		
37	Public Domain (International Institute of Social History)	**102-103**	Public Domain		
		104-105	© AFP/Getty Images		
		106	National Archives		